Gothic Life

THE ESSENTIAL GUIDE TO MACABRE STYLE

Aurelio Voltaire

EPIC INK

Contents

Preface: A Letter to the Reader

Hello, my spooky friend!

My name is Aurelio Voltaire and I've been living what you could call a "spooky lifestyle" for several decades now. What does that mean? Well, if a so-called "normal person" were to see me walking down the street, they might think to themselves, "Hmm . . . that guy looks like a vampire."

If I were to invite them into my home, they'd barely make it one step into the Lair of Voltaire before blurting out, "Oh, God, he's *definitely* a vampire! Run!"

As someone who absolutely adores horror, Halloween, monsters, and the macabre, I've spent years transforming every aspect of my life—from what I wear to how I decorate my home—into a cozy little world where every day is Halloween and a ghoul like me can feel right at home any time of year. I've done everything I can to transform my little New York apartment into a lair worthy of darkside royalty.

Since 2016, when the first episode of my YouTube show, *Gothic Homemaking*, went live, I've explored countless ways to decorate my lair, from painting walls black, to building Gothic furniture, to sourcing skulls and skeletons. I've traveled to the ends of the world in search of oddities, dark art, and macabre objets d'art. I've scoured the Halloween offerings of all the major chain stores year after year for that

Sticks and stones may break my bones, but at least then I'll have some great new decor!

special piece that would fit perfectly in the lair of an actual vampire. Moreover, I've created scores of DIY projects, where I've used readily found objects and supplies to create decorations for my lair, steeped in Gothic aesthetic. And since my lair started as a mere studio apartment, you do not need to own a Victorian mansion to use these techniques. You'll be able to get right to transforming your lair whether you live in a spacious castle or a tiny dorm room.

When I'm not hosting *Gothic Homemaking*, I'm a touring musician, singing some of my most dastardly ditties, including songs I wrote for the Cartoon Network show, *The Grim Adventures of Billy & Mandy*, and for the viral *Vampair* series by Daria Cohen. On stage, I ask audiences how it's possible that a grown man has come to a place in his life where he strives to dress like a Disney villain. My half-joking answer is that if they think a "difficult childhood" had something to do with it, they might be on to something!

The truth is, there is no one correct or predetermined path to becoming a person who is obsessed with Halloween, who loves Gothic culture, or who can't get enough of dark decor. In my case, as I know is the case for many of us, I was faced with quite a lot of darkness as a child. Perhaps hoping to understand this "darkness," I went in search of it. I discovered horror films. I fell in love with vampire lore. I developed a passion for Halloween, and, ultimately, I found my way to the Gothic subculture. The "darkness" I found, the one you will encounter in this book, is a wonderful and, I might add, completely harmless fascination with a certain eerie and romantic aesthetic.

When I was seventeen, I ran away from home and moved to New York, where I was lucky enough to get work as a stop-motion animator. During that time, I made countless props and miniature sets, and many of the techniques I picked up along the way I still use in my dark decor projects to this day. I'll be sharing some of those techniques with you in this book!

In addition to my stop-motion work and a foray into creator-owned comic books, I also learned to play the guitar and started writing and recording music. Since then, I have toured the world several times over, singing songs that are, like most of what I do, simultaneously dark and spooky and lighthearted and joyous. I make my *Gothic Homemaking* episodes to share the tremendous pleasure it gives me to transform my tiny home into a Gothic lair, while helping others to do the same. And I do my very best to share this love I have for the macabre, a love that ironically brings so much light into my life!

Since my first seventeen years on this planet were filled with pain and sadness and being told my interests were weird and unacceptable, my goal is to fill the rest of my days with happiness. For me, that means allowing myself to indulge in all the "dark" aesthetics I love so much and living my life by my own rules, as ooky and spooky as it may seem to others.

But, most importantly, it brings me immense joy to be able to share this spooky happiness with *you*. It is my sincere hope that through this book I will be able to help you live *your* best Gothic life!

Just one glorious corner of the Lair's living room.

Part 1
Welcome to Your Spooky Life

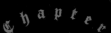

1

Discovering Your Gothic Self

While I live my spooky lifestyle 24/7, 365 days a year, most people don't embrace the macabre until Halloween rolls around. As a musician, my number of monthly listeners on Spotify jumps up drastically in October, as people suddenly remember spooky songs of mine that they'd like to add to their Halloween playlist. I eventually realized that to many people I'm "that Halloween guy" who makes "the Halloween music." The same is true of *Gothic Homemaking*, my show on YouTube. Views dramatically rise in the ramp-up to October and Halloween . . . and then they drop to normal levels once Thanksgiving rears its horribly wholesome face. The idea that hordes of people

don't think to enjoy your work until a particular holiday rolls around might offend some creators. Not me!

In 2022, during one of those October surges, my humble homemaking show managed to catch the attention of the *New York Times*, who did a story on it and referred to me as "the Martha Stewart for macabre homemakers," as well as "a lifestyle guru for people who embrace spookiness in all seasons." In the over 100 episodes of *Gothic Homemaking*, I've covered creepy cooking, devilish drinks and desserts, spooky travel destinations, places to buy wicked wares, and of course many macabre DIY projects to creepify every corner of a crypt. I still have much more in my arsenal to offer, and it gives me tremendous pleasure to be able to share my decorating and spooky lifestyle tips with you in this book!

My hope is that you'll find, within the pages of this tiny tome, all you will need to live your best spooky life, including tips on when and where to find dark decor items that will transform your space into a proper Gothic lair. You'll also see DIY projects where I've transformed boring household items from the mundane to the macabre. I will share with you some of my favorite drink and food recipes for when you are ready to entertain the creatures of the night in your own, amazing space. I'll show you how to add a bit of creepiness to any holiday, and how to make the very best of the spookiest night of the year, Halloween. And I will share with you from whence and from whom I find inspiration. It is my goal that you will be able to use this book to inspire your own journey through the macabre.

There are some simple boxes you can check to create a basic Gothic space (and I will certainly be showing you those!), but the sky is truly the limit on how far you can take it. The more you deviate from the expected, the more unique and personal your home will be. A black-on-black lair full of coffin-shaped everything is great, believe me, but if there is a color you love, use it! You say you're partial to nautical themes? Skeletal mermaids? Killer robots? Psychotic clowns and haunted dolls? Invite them in! Perhaps your style is closer to pastel Goth or Dark Academia. Or perhaps you wish to create a Halloween home where it's always the spookiest time of year. I can give you the tools you'll need to get started, but ultimately your lair must serve one purpose above all others: it must be a place you want to come home to, where you feel happy, comfortable, and surrounded by the colors, shapes, and motifs you love.

PREVIOUS:
Welcome to the
Lair of Voltaire.

OPPOSITE: Just
some of the many
darkly delightful
pieces you can
learn to create!

I always say that in Gothic homemaking there are no mistakes. Many interior designers would likely disagree with me, but that's because they're looking at things academically. Creating a Gothic lair isn't about rules and equations, it's about emotions. If a color scheme you've chosen makes you smile (no matter how much someone tells you it isn't "Gothic"), or an item you purchased or made makes you feel like you're finally living in the home of your dreams, then you've clearly chosen wisely! The one and only barometer for how your lair is coming along is *you* and how *you* feel in your space. All the tips in this book are designed to provide a point from which to jump. You can use them exactly as they are or add your own spin to create the haunted home of your dreams.

Living a spooky life means different things to different people. If you're coming from or are particularly interested in the Goth scene (such as the dark music scene pioneered by bands like Bauhaus, The Cure, Siouxsie and the Banshees, etc.), then you'll likely want to decorate liberally with black and with motifs such as skulls, coffins, and bats. Steampunk and Dark Academia are close relatives of the Gothic look, and you can dip your toe into one of those, with a darker twist. If you love Halloween, work orange into your color scheme and try out some jack-o'-lanterns, witches, and ghosts. If you're into Victorian antiquity, try washed-out colors, distressed surfaces, old lace, and creepy dolls. Perhaps medical oddities are your thing and you wish to transform your space into a cross between a mad scientist's lab and an old museum, complete with jarred specimens, books, and sepia tones. Or maybe you wish to create an H. P. Lovecraft-inspired, cosmic-horror-themed home in black and rich greens, with tentacles bursting from every wall. Apparently, I was wrong before—even the sky *isn't* the limit!

A spooky lifestyle could be firmly rooted in the Goth subculture of the '80s, its music, its fashion, and its aesthetics. Or it could be just about anything that celebrates the ooky, the spooky, the uncanny, or the macabre. The underlying principle of a Gothic life is that instead of dressing and surrounding yourself in the "normal," there is something about your aesthetics that brings to mind things that are morbid, macabre, dark, romantic, or whimsically spooky. The trick is to find out exactly what kind of spooky life is for you. If people around you are constantly telling you your style is creepy, weird, disturbing, scary, spooky, frightening, or downright horrifying, chances are you are already

living a wonderfully spooky life. If you're still on the path to finding your way to that place, simply ask yourself what makes you happy. Is it bats? Is it snakes? Perhaps it's the head that you found in the lake?

Together, we will discover exactly what kind of home you wish to create for yourself and then, using the concepts and techniques I share in this book, we are going to build you the Gothic lair you've always dreamed of!

Murder, She Crowed cushions from my Society 6 store.

2

Guided by Glorious Ghouls

We are all influenced, whether we realize it or not, by the things we see and the people we meet. As a teenager, singers like David Bowie, and Gary Numan and Richard Butler of the Psychedelic Furs, showed me that it was okay for a man to wear makeup. Adam Ant showed me it was okay to dress like a pirate, and David Vanian of The Damned showed me it was okay to dress like a vampire—which is probably how I ended up looking like an undead pirate (a vampirate?). In some way, their mere existence gave me *permission* to explore my own identity. This chapter covers just a few of the artists and performers who have embraced a deliciously dark lifestyle and inspired me and so many others to do the same.

Screamin' Jay Hawkins

Born in 1929, this singer was known for his over-the-top, theatrical performances, during which he'd emerge from a coffin on stage, often holding a skull-topped cane or other voodoo props. Coupled with his operatic form of singing, which included lots of grunts and groans, Hawkins is largely regarded as one of the first (if not *the* first) shock-rocker. He's best known for his song "I Put a Spell on You," and has inspired artists like Alice Cooper, The Cramps, Black Sabbath, Rob Zombie, Glenn Danzig, and Marilyn Manson. Hawkins was one of the first to use macabre or morbid stage props to create a Gothic persona on stage. Moreover, he introduced to the genre the image of the voodoo witch doctor as a Gothic archetype.

Cab Calloway

This American jazz singer and bandleader was a regular performer at the famed Cotton Club in Harlem, New York, beginning in 1931. Originally hired to substitute for Duke Ellington while Ellington was on tour, Calloway and his band became so popular he was given a

permanent position there. In 1931, he recorded his biggest hit, "Minnie the Moocher," which was the first single by a Black American to sell a million copies. Calloway also performed three hit songs in the Betty Boop cartoons of the 1930s. Using a technique called rotoscoping, the Max Fleischer animation company filmed Calloway doing his trademark dances and then used that footage as inspiration for the movements of the animated monsters in the cartoons. Being a monster kid, I loved those cartoons growing up, and I clearly wasn't the only one: Danny Elfman was inspired by Calloway's work when writing "Oogie Boogie's Song" for *The Nightmare Before Christmas.*

Peter Murphy

Few would disagree that Bauhaus frontman Peter Murphy paved
the way for the Gothic rock genre. Lean and ghostly pale (and often
performing shirtless), Murphy would emerge from abject darkness into
a harsh white light looking like Cesare, the somnambulist from the
German expressionistic film, *The Cabinet of Dr. Caligari.* His handsome,
chiseled features cast dark shadows in the hollows of his cheeks that
complimented his jet-black hair and black eyeliner. While the rest of the
world seemed to be in color, somehow Peter Murphy always seemed to
be in black and white. Bauhaus is perhaps best known for creating the
undisputed anthem of the Gothrock movement, "Bela Lugosi's Dead."

Siouxsie Sioux

Post-punk goddess Siouxsie Sioux, the lead singer of
Siouxsie and the Banshees, was not only a musical
pioneer but a style icon as well. Taking elements of
punk aesthetics and adding a heavy dose of black,
Siouxsie sported the prototypical Goth look for
women early in the Gothic movement. The torn
fishnets, studded leather bracelets, and black leather
boots of punk were all in place, as was spiky black hair
that looked like it might scratch the sky. And then
there was the makeup! Her thick, black, cat eye was
so dramatic and bold, it summoned images of Kabuki
performers or an Egyptian god of the underworld.
Before Goth diverged into a million different styles,
every girl in the scene wanted to look like Siouxsie.
Standout hits by Siouxsie and the Banshees include
"Cities in Dust," "Spellbound," and "Peek-A-Boo," all
of which are Goth club dancefloor favorites.

Siouxsie Sioux
performs in London
in December 1982.

Robert Smith

Once a member of Siouxsie and the Banshees, Robert Smith skyrocketed
to fame as the lead singer of The Cure. His back-combed, giant rat's nest
of hair and trademark messy red lipstick are instantly recognizable and
staples of the Gothic aesthetic. Unlike the sleek, form-fitting vampiric
fashions or elegant Victorian frocks sometimes favored by men in the

Gothic world, Smith often opted for sneakers and baggy sweaters or T-shirts, proving you don't need to be fussy to be Gothic. Smith's music also diverges from a lot of the Gothic fray. Sometimes leaning into nearly pop melodies and arrangements, The Cure are quite likely the band from the Gothic rock scene with the broadest appeal.

Edgar Allan Poe

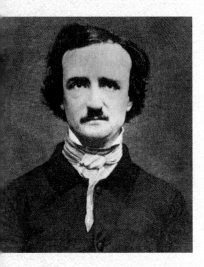

No other American author is more associated with the Gothic movement than Edgar Allan Poe. This nineteenth-century writer and poet penned some of the most famous horror stories, from "The Raven" to "The Tell-Tale Heart," and stories like "The Fall of the House of Usher," "The Pit and the Pendulum," and "The Masque of the Red Death" have been realized as films or TV series. Engaging with a Poe story or poem makes you want to envelop yourself in these dark, romantic images, and, luckily, you can. His legacy endures, even long after his death, like a heart beating under the floorboards. In the 1980s, the "RomantiGoth" or "Victorian Goth" style began to take hold and eventually become the norm in the scene. I wonder if the work of Edgar Allan Poe wasn't somewhat responsible for that.

ABOVE: Edgar Allan Poe, author of many short stories that spooked you in high school.

RIGHT: Vincent Price in a publicity still for the film *The Bat* (1959)—how fitting!

Vincent Price

Price started his career in the late 1930s as a character actor, and by the 1950s he was often appearing in horror films. With leading roles in such horror hits as *House of Wax*, *The Fly*, and *House on Haunted Hill*, Price became a household name and something of a god to monster kids obsessed with horror. During his career, Price starred in many films based on Poe's works, including *House of Usher*, *The Pit and the Pendulum*, *The Masque of the Red Death*, and *The Raven*. He later lent his voice to Alice Cooper's song "The Black Widow" and Michael Jackson's "Thriller." In 1982, Price also provided the narration to the stop-motion film *Vincent*, made by a young

filmmaker named Tim Burton. Price also had a style and grace all his own, with crisp, clear diction, ramrod straight posture, and a tie or ascot around his neck. His villains were smart, witty, perhaps supercilious, sarcastic, sinister, and always sophisticated. And as Price grew older, he showed us that a spooky life has no age limits.

Tim Burton

No one has done more to bring Gothic aesthetics to mainstream Hollywood than Tim Burton. Take away the scissors and Edward Scissorhands, with his pasty white face and shiny black leather clothes, would be right at home lurching around the dancefloor at a local Goth night. Burton's frequent use of an extremely limited color palette (basically grayscale) and the reoccurrence of morbid themes, cemeteries, gargoyles, wrought-iron fences, and all those barren, twisty trees in his work create a style that's come to be known as "Burtonesque." Truth be told, it's just Gothic. The fact that he typically wears all black and looks like he goes to the same hair salon as Robert Smith would indicate he's a card-carrying member of the Goth crowd.

Jenna Ortega as Wednesday Addams in the Netflix series *Wednesday* (2022–).

Wednesday Addams

There is no doubt in my mind that there are thousands of young girls watching *Wednesday* on Netflix and becoming extremely curious about the Gothic lifestyle. And I only hope their parents will understand that once you look past all the dark imagery, Wednesday is someone to look up to. She is strong, smart, creative, talented, and clever and, above all, she's no one's fool. In a lot of ways, she's an amazing role model for a young lady. (I'm choosing to overlook the sadistic, homicidal tendencies for the moment.) She has spooky pets and fascinating hobbies, from playing the cello to fencing to solving mysteries, and her relationship with her parents is unusual, in that they don't treat her like a daughter who must do as they say. Wednesday is confident and accomplished, and her cynical outlook and witty one-liners also make her extremely entertaining to watch. She also has Hispanic heritage—another plus! For so many young Hispanic girls, Wednesday demonstrates that this spooky lifestyle is just as much for them as it is for anyone else.

Wesley Snipes as Blade, making trench coats look cool since 1998.

Blade

Blade is a Marvel superhero who first appeared in *The Tomb of Dracula* #10 in 1973. He is a dhampir (a mythical creature who is part human and part vampire) who must not be too fond of one of his parents, because he's sworn to rid the entire world of vampires. He is, simply put, a badass vampire hunter. Blade was first brought to the big screen in 1998, with Wesley Snipes in the titular role. Snipes played the character two more times in subsequent sequels. Unlike a lot of characters from vampire lore, Blade does not wear flamboyant or fancy dress from the eighteenth or nineteenth centuries. Blade is typically depicted in modern, urban, practically militaristic or tactical clothing, featuring a long black trench coat, black body armor, and lots of tight, shiny black leather. It's a modern masculine look, to be certain. He's also typically armed to the teeth (or is that fangs?). I see a great many people in the Goth scene who find inspiration in this character's masculine, athletic, and ominous style.

Vampira

Maila Nurmi was a young actress of Finnish descent who traveled to Hollywood seeking fame and fortune in the early 1950s. But the only work she was able to find was as a pin-up model. Determined to be discovered, Nurmi attended a masquerade ball full of movers and shakers in a costume she hoped would make an impression. Inspired by the Addams Family cartoons in *The New Yorker*, she based her costume on Morticia, donning a tight black dress with a plunging neckline and long, tattered bell sleeves. She painted her face a ghastly white and sported jet-black, angular eyebrows and long, raven-black hair.

The costume was a success. Nurmi was contacted by a producer at local Los Angeles TV station KABC-TV, who offered her a job introducing mostly low-budget horror films late at night. Not wanting to play Morticia without the consent of the character's creator, Charles Addams, Nurmi developed a character of her own named Vampira. Familiar with the bondage magazines of the day, from which Nurmi purchased her corsets, she decided to add a dominatrix touch to her outfit. She created a dark, brooding, and sexy vampire vixen that spoke in macabre puns and mocked the films she was showcasing. The first-ever horror host was born!

Maila Nurmi in all her glorious Vampira regalia.

The Vampira Show ran for just over a year, from 1954 to 1955. In that time, *Life* magazine did a five-page spread on her and she appeared with Bela Lugosi and Lon Chaney, Jr. on the wildly popular *The Red Skeleton Hour*. And then, after her show's cancellation, Nurmi never worked as Vampira again—except in a cameo in the Ed Wood film, *Plan 9 from Outer Space*. Though she has no lines, it is the role for which she is ironically best known. Vampira mixed dark, Gothic aesthetics with fetish-scene sex appeal, creating a creature that inspires to this day.

Elvira, Mistress of the Dark

There is likely no other spooky personality alive in the world today who is as well known as Elvira. This curvaceous, bawdy-joke-cracking vampire vixen is the creation of American actress Cassandra Peterson. Peterson created the character in the early 1980s to play the host of KHJ-TV's *Elvira's Movie Macabre*. That show was originally meant to be a reboot of *The Vampira Show*, with Maila Nurmi acting as executive producer, but Nurmi left the project due to creative differences. In the spirit of other horror hosts like Zacherley and Vampira, Elvira would introduce B-horror movies and then make them more entertaining by making quips during the film or during

short breaks. The popularity of the show led to two feature films, a TV show, and a line of merchandise that continues to grow even forty years later.

Peterson has said her character's looks were inspired by Morticia. Featuring a long, tight-fitting black dress and plenty of cleavage, Elvira's personality was far from the serious vampiric seductress the world was used to. Cassandra Peterson created Elvira while part of the improv group the Groundlings, basing her on the stereotype of the "valley girl." She turned the bawdiness way, way up and gave Elvira a wise-cracking, flirtatious personality. Elvira brought the spooky scene something it lacked: a much-needed laugh!

The delightfully frightful folks chosen for this list each brought something different and unique to the Gothic aesthetic. In doing so, they expanded the definition of what it meant to be Gothic and also showed us *who* can participate. While the stereotypical image of the Goth might be a young, pasty-faced person in white face makeup dressed in Victorian vampire garb, I hope these examples prove that a spooky lifestyle is for *everyone*. Whether you're young or old, secular or religious, local or foreign, light- or dark-skinned, thick or thin, you are welcome here!

And for those who tell you that you don't belong or that you're "not doing it right," I say this: the Goth scene (and, by extension, other spooky scenes) is a living, breathing organism made of hundreds of thousands (possibly millions) of human beings who contribute their own ideas to the scene. No one person can say what is or isn't Gothic, they can only say what it is or isn't to *them*. Whether you like to dress like Siouxsie Sioux in torn fishnets and spiky hair, like Blade with his militaristic, buff bravado, or like a vampire in velvet from a bygone era, I can assure you that if you delight in how you've styled yourself and it helps you feel like you've become the person you've always wanted to be, then you are indeed doing it right! And you might very well be the one creating the next Gothic trend.

Having said all of that, dressing like any of the style icons above is liable to raise some eyebrows among the common folk. Therefore, it's important to have a certain mindset. Know that you have a right to be whoever you want to be. Furthermore, you are not bothering anyone by looking interesting or unique and by living as your authentic self. If people have a problem with that, it's their problem, not yours.

It's important to me that people realize that we spooky folks are kind, intelligent, creative, respectful, and productive members of society. When I'm at the receiving end of some hatred or aggression, I lean on the confidence I have that I am exactly who I want to be and that I have a right to be this person. And when all else fails and they simply can't understand why I'm dressed the way I'm dressed, to quote one of my songs, "I just look them in the eye and tell them I was Raised by Bats!"

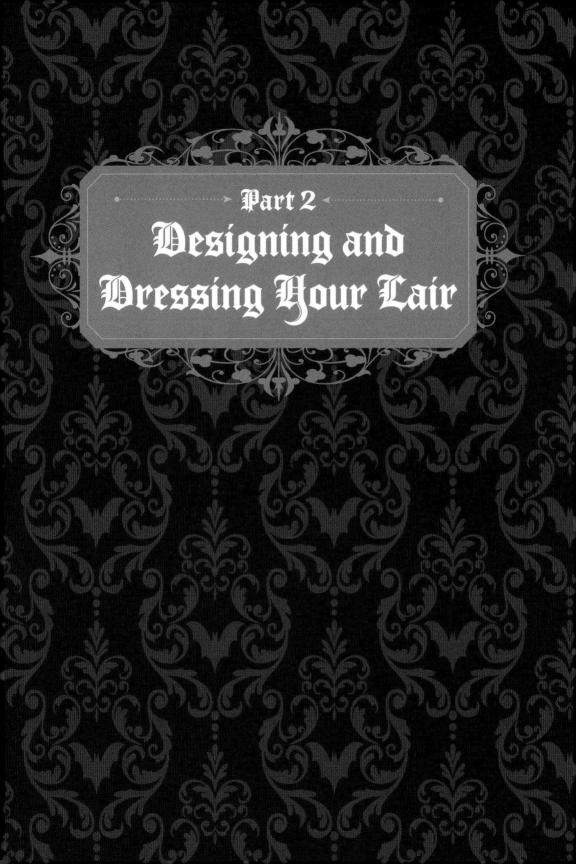

Part 2
Designing and Dressing Your Lair

3

Creating a
Gothic Home

ow that we've talked about some of the glorious ghouls who inspire us, we can apply our inspiration to interior decorating. Before you dive in, make a list of some of your favorite spooky folks and aesthetics. Flip through Pinterest or Instagram and you'll find no shortage of accounts dedicated to Gothic and Halloween home decor. Follow those accounts! Save or screenshot posts of homes that make you think, *I wish I lived there*, and in time you will have a mountain of ideas to help inspire you. I also take note when watching horror films or period pieces where the action is taking place in a space that is simply to die for.

Once you have a bank of images like these, take a moment to see if there are any trends in what you've saved that might inform the direction in which you wish to go. Are most of the walls painted black in the images you've collected? Are most of the images of Victorian interiors? Are there lots of shots of sepia-toned rooms full of oddities? The answers to these questions can give you a good base to build from. Keep in mind that you don't need to copy a home you've seen or stick to a very specific theme. In the end, the goal is to gather everything that's inspired you, pick and choose what works for you, and discard the rest. And if there are specific elements you wish to include or an image of your entire home that exists nowhere but in your own imagination, even better! Make collages, sketch it out, journal on what you want your future home to look like. The goal is to create a place that you will be happy in, no matter what the palette or guiding aesthetic, and if you do that, you'll likely create a lair that is uniquely you.

My humble little hovel (and believe me when I say it was exactly that when I moved in twenty years ago) was an empty, eleven-by-thirteen-foot studio apartment in New York City's East Village. When I first moved in, I had fallen on some hard financial times and was desperate to find a place I could afford. At $1,000 a month the place was considered a steal, even back in 2002. Moreover, the place was rent-stabilized, meaning the landlord could not raise the rent more than two percent per year. And if you're wondering why I'm still here two decades later, well, to rent an identical apartment in my neighborhood would now cost more than double what I currently pay.

Not everyone will understand why we New Yorkers are willing to pay so much money to live in such tiny spaces. But for some of us, the idea of being in the center of the universe is exhilarating. Over the years, I've enjoyed stepping out the front door of my home and strolling to see *The Phantom of the Opera* or *Beetlejuice* on Broadway. I'm steps away from 35,000 of the world's best restaurants and some of the world's finest museums. All the biggest bands come through New York City. You're also probably not going to run into David Bowie (RIP), Keith Richards, or Björk while walking down the street in a small town, but in New York I have run into them all . . . multiple times!

Still, living in a tiny space can be extremely frustrating, which is why you really have to make it your own. I can show you how to do that, and since my place is so small, you can rest assured that these tips

PREVIOUS: This Devil throne is a fairly new addition to the Lair. When the throne that was originally there finally breathed its last breath, I decided to upgrade to a sinister seat that really gives me wings.

LEFT: This hallway beckons you deeper into the Lair.

will work for a space of any size. Whether you own or rent, you'll find ideas in this book that will help you create your lair . . . and *re-create* your lair, when the time comes!

In the two decades I've lived in my apartment, I've transformed the space twice. The first time was documented in a book of mine called *Paint it Black: A Guide to Gothic Homemaking*, which was the inspiration for my show, *Gothic Homemaking*. In that incarnation, the Lair had red walls and black furniture. Compared to how it looks now, it was practically a minimalist Gothic space.

ABOVE: This is the
south-facing wall of
the Lair. I jokingly
tell people I have
two thrones and
no kingdoms.

OPPOSITE: This is
the corner of the
Lair that went viral.
It is perhaps the
most-often-seen
part, as it serves
as the backdrop
for the show.

In 2016, when I embarked on making *Gothic Homemaking* for YouTube, I gutted the space and started over. What works for you at one point in your life might not work forever, so it's important to remain open to changes big and small. Ideally, you want your living space to *always* be an exciting and comfortable place for you to live in.

You might be surprised to know that I did not have a theme in mind when I created the Lair as it exists today. Instead, what I had was a handful of random ideas and specific items I knew I wanted to incorporate. I knew I wanted to start with gray walls and that I wanted to put up ornate ceiling tiles. I had an idea to cover the walls with vinyl decals of barren branches. I knew I wanted to furnish the space with Gothic thrones adorned with intricate baroque woodwork. I longed to have ravens perched on human skulls resting on ornate wall sconces. In other words, I just wanted to be surrounded by things I loved and was excited about. One by one, as

RIGHT: This Raised by Bats throne was originally designed and created specifically for me by Australian Gothic furniture company, Haunt.

OPPOSITE: This coffin-shaped armoire, made for the episode "Wardrobe of the Damned," holds all of my fancy frocks.

I added each element, I simply nipped and tucked and adjusted until they fit together in a way that worked for me, a process I documented in the first season of *Gothic Homemaking*.

After a season or two of *Gothic Homemaking*, it was pointed out to me that a photo of my apartment that I'd posted on social media had gone viral as an ideal Gothic home. I was really delighted that the space I'd created to make myself feel happy brought joy and inspiration to others as well. I also wondered how many of the people who saw that photo realized they were practically looking at the entire space . . . or just how many disasters I encountered before the space came to look that way.

The fact is, it isn't always going to go smoothly. And that's okay. It's part of the process. Making mistakes is how we learn to do better or how we discover that we're heading in the wrong direction and need to reset our course. I assure you, there were certainly many mistakes in the creation of my own personal Lair. For one, those gray walls I wanted turned out to be lavender on the first try! (More on that in Chapter 4.) I learned the hard way that using a harsh soap to clean the Bats and Beasts wallpaper I have hanging in my Gothic bathroom can take the design clean off. And I've lost count how much flesh I've shed to hot glue gun mishaps. But once everything comes together, the successes will far outweigh the failures.

One of my first DIY furniture projects on the show was the Haunted Library End Table. This piece consists of four resin skulls holding up a column of books, atop which rests a framed Ouija board. I've never had a project start out so disastrously! At one point, all my skulls were broken, soaked in wet cement and ruined. And yet, after a bit of perseverance (and a willingness to start again from scratch), I managed to finish the project, and it is still my absolute favorite piece I've ever made.

My lair is truly a labor of love. I created it specifically so I would have a place I'd actually want to come home to and a place I could feel proud entertaining in (even if it's the size of many people's pantries), and I feel that I ended up with a unique look. And because the only design rule I follow is that *my* space should make *me* happy, I think I can call it a great success. Allow me to give you a short tour.

The Lair of Voltaire is a work in progress. Everything in the space exists for one purpose: to create a home I can feel comfortable, happy, and fulfilled in. When I look around, I sense that I'm in a space that reflects who I am, and should a time come when that is no longer the case, I will change an item here or there until it does. At the end of the day, if someone feels this particular style is not right for them or a delivery person walks in and thinks my place "looks like spook house," all that matters is whether I feel at home in my Lair Sweet Lair.

ABOVE: The latest addition to the Lair is the creation of my Gothic kitchen. Read on to see the spooky meals I create here!

OPPOSITE: I've collected some devilishly beautiful art to create this gallery wall.

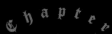

4

The Basics of Dark Decor

ow that you've seen my humble home of horrors, it's time to dive in and work on yours! In this section, I'm going to start with the very basic building blocks of dark decor. We are going to cover some color choices that will instantly set the right mood for your space, discuss some of the iconography of the spooky scene, talk about some wall treatments that will create the framework for your dark den, and lay the foundation upon which you can build a lair of your very own. But first, I feel it's important that we start with defining a term that we'll use a lot in the process. And that term is Gothic.

What is Goth?

The Lair of Voltaire could colloquially be referred to as a "Gothic apartment." There is conspicuous use of the color black and motifs often associated with the Gothic lifestyle, such as skulls, bats, and coffins. But the word Gothic has been mangled and misused for so many centuries that I think I need to define it before we can properly embark on a conversation about dark aesthetics.

The word *Gothic* literally refers to a Germanic tribe in the first century called the Goths. The Goths were likely considered uncivilized barbarians by many of their contemporaries, so in the fourth or fifth century, when the Goths did the unthinkable and toppled the Roman Empire, it was *simply barbaric*! And so the word *Gothic* came to be associated with the word *barbaric*.

The Goths, having sacked the seat of modern civilization, ushered in what is commonly known as the Middle Ages or Dark Ages. In this time, castles sprung up all over Europe, strongholds built to protect royals and their courts. These structures were typically large, thick, stone buildings made in a Germanic style. Designed to keep enemies out, they also had a habit of not letting much light in!

Fast forward to the Renaissance. Between the fourteenth and sixteenth centuries there was a renewed interest in the classical architecture and knowledge of ancient Greece and Rome. Artists and architects of that time showed their disdain for the "rude" Germanic structures of the Dark Ages by labeling them "Gothic," referring to those uncivilized and unenlightened barbarians that ended all that was good in Rome centuries before, and the name *Gothic architecture* has remained to this day.

The start of the Romantic movement in the eighteenth century brought a reevaluation of the Dark Ages. Artists and philosophers of the time looked to explore humanity's deepest, darkest desires to better understand the human condition, resulting in novels like Mary Shelley's *Frankenstein* and Bram Stoker's *Dracula,* as well as the works of Edgar Allan Poe.

With the later advent of motion pictures, some of these Gothic horror books were adapted, giving us some of the most famous of the classic horror films of the 1930s. Half a century later, in the mid-1970s, punk rock music was born, and in time it spawned an offshoot called post-punk that was more introspective and experimental. Bands like

Siouxsie and the Banshees, The Cure, and Joy Division made music often characterized as melancholy and occasionally morbid, echoing themes found in Gothic literature. When the band Bauhaus directly referenced a vampire film with their song "Bela Lugosi's Dead" in 1979, they ushered in the Gothic rock genre.

When I speak of my decorating style, rather than use the term *Gothic* (so as not to have you think I'm referring solely to the musical sub-genre, however much I love it), I prefer *dark decor*. It's an umbrella term that I feel encompasses all things wonderfully macabre and wickedly morbid, things that will allow you to create your own home sweet haunted home.

Let's fly, my pretties!

𝔓𝔞𝔦𝔫𝔱 𝔦𝔱 𝔅𝔩𝔞𝔠𝔨

Black is the color of night, a time that frightens most and exhilarates some. If there's one thing I've learned in my decades of dark decorating, it's that if you paint something black, you are *transforming* it. When I've glued a bunch of random odds and ends onto, say, a wooden picture frame, creating a seemingly chaotic project, all I need do is press down on the nozzle of a can of black lacquer spray paint to transform it into a glorious, unified frame fit for the portrait of a long-dead countess hanging on the walls of Castle Dracula. (See page 67 for spray-painting tips.)

My spooky friend, *that* is the power of painting things black!

In transforming your home, ask yourself what you can paint black. Perhaps it's a figurine or statuette, a piece of furniture like an armoire, or some picture frames. Visit a thrift store or antique shop and find some items that have beautiful shapes and paint them black to match your dark aesthetic. Items that look particularly good painted black are those with a Victorian design or a lot of Baroque detail. Avoid modern, sleek items with few details and smooth surfaces.

PREVIOUS: Birds of a dark feather adorn my walls together.

BELOW: See what wonders you can create with some black spray paint?

A convincing
replica skull to
spice up any shelf.

Black is also not the only color you can use to create your spooky lair. But since we're tackling the very basics of dark decor, it's the obvious place to start. We will discuss some other color schemes on pages 51-53.

Sinister Symbols for a Macabre Mood

Liberal use of the color black is a great way to immediately create a Gothic feel. Another is the use of Gothic iconography, including many simple symbols and motifs you can use to achieve that goal.

The Sardonic Smile of Death

There is no image that better communicates that yours is indeed a den of darkness than a human skull. For centuries, skulls have symbolized danger, warning people that a substance might be poisonous or that an area they are entering might lead to their untimely deaths.

Place a sticker of a skull on a bottle painted black and you instantly transform it from a regular wine bottle to something a vampirate might swig from.

Around Halloween time, you'll find no shortage of resin skulls and skeletons that will really help to create a creepy corner in your cave. Outside spooky season, try visiting an oddities market or searching art sites online like Etsy.

And of course, if you're a true connoisseur, you can own a real human skull to make sure all who enter know you mean business! Do your research to find natural history and oddities stores that specialize in selling ethically and legally sourced human skulls and skeletons.

Release the Bats!

Another symbol that will immediately conjure up the Gothic is the bat. Bats are nocturnal, venturing forth when most mortals prefer to be safe in their beds. And of course, the infamous vampire bat drinks blood. The great irony is that vampire bats make up just a tiny percentage of all the bats on Earth, and even vampire bats prefer to feed on the blood of livestock.

Bats are timid. They are nocturnal. They tend to stay away from humans and prefer the company of other bats. Because of their spooky appearance, they are needlessly feared by many but are in essence harmless and, in fact, great to have around. Come to think of it . . . they are just like Goths!

A wooden bat carving from Bali.

A good place to start with a bat motif is with some art. Frame some paintings or prints that feature bats and hang them on your walls. Bat figurines or bat-adorned sculptures are also a great way to let people know that you are a vampire bat yourself . . . or just love sky puppies!

Coffin-shaped Everything

Another image that strikes fear into the hearts of most but is beloved in dark-decorating circles is the coffin. While there are different types, the one that gets the most attention is the six-sided toe-pincher coffin, widest where the shoulders of the corpse would be and narrowest at the feet. The shape is instantly recognizable—the moment your eyes fall upon a coffin, you know you are looking at a box for a dead person.

I have a six-foot-tall coffin-shaped armoire in the Lair of Voltaire for all my frightful frocks. I designed some smaller coffin-shaped cabinets in which I keep everything from spices in my kitchen to Gothic glassware in my living room (or is that my dying room?). I have a coffin-shaped utensil holder for my smaller kitchen utensils, a coffin-shaped incense burner in my bathroom, and three hundred miniature wooden coffins in my closet that I haven't figured out what to do with yet! I drink from a coffin-shaped flask and eat my meals on a coffin-shaped tray. You get the picture.

Bubble, Bubble, Toil, and Trouble

Go to any home goods store during the spookiest time of year and you'll find plenty of cartoony witch-themed items. But the iconography of witches also finds itself in dark decor through, well . . . real witches! Namely, members of the Pagan and Wiccan communities who might refer to themselves as witches.

Whether it's the green Halloween witches with noses covered in warts or the Wiccan witches of the real world, one thing is for certain—there

LEFT: Whether you use it to set the right spooky mood or to hold your spare change, you can't go wrong with these skeletons holding cauldrons.

BELOW: Corvids and craniums go together like brimstone and treacle.

will be cauldrons! You can find them in a variety of materials, from ceramic to plastic to metal.

I have a ton of cauldrons in my home, mostly in my Gothic kitchen. I even use small ceramic cauldrons for serving desserts. But we'll get into that later in the book, when we start to entertain some ghosts and goblins in the Lair (see page 95).

Quoth the Raven, "Evermore!"

If there is a Gothic bird on this planet, that bird is the raven. It's black, it's ominous, and its harsh and mournful cry sounds like a warning of impending doom. The raven, immortalized by Poe in his famous poem, has long been associated with death and darkness. In Swedish lore, ravens are thought to be the souls of murdered people not given a proper Christian burial. In other cultures, they are

perceived as dark omens. A member of the corvid family, the raven is related to, and shares a fair amount of attributes with, its smaller cousin, the crow. Just as beguiling, the crow inspired James O'Barr to create a Gothic anti-hero in his comic book (and subsequent film) series, *The Crow*.

A group of ravens is called *an unkindness*, while a group of crows is referred to as *a murder*. It's no surprise these birds have a special place in the Gothic world!

When the Halloween season rolls around, you can find many raven- and crow-related decorative items to add to your lair. There are resin statues available with a raven perched atop a tombstone, skull, or stack of books, perhaps directly referencing Poe's poem. You'll find no shortage of Styrofoam figures covered in black feathers but, try as they may, I have never seen one that looked even remotely realistic. This is why I prefer real taxidermy.

If you prefer non-organic raven decorations, fear not! There are many vegan options out there, such as throw pillows that feature those fierce feathered fiends. I might also suggest some raven art for your walls or some vinyl decals of those wicked winged ones.

Ironically, these candelabras bring a touch of darkness into your home.

Let There Be Light

I shall never forget the image of Bela Lugosi descending those grandiose stairs in the original *Dracula* film, holding a candelabra in his pale hand. And what soul who ever had the pleasure of seeing the musical version of *The Phantom of the Opera* will ever forget when those wrought-iron candelabras rose from the sewers of Paris and magically lit themselves?

Sure, the electric light is a wonderful invention, but add a candelabra or two to your home and people will instantly know they've entered a room full of dark romance.

A Note on Taxidermy

While I'm not here to impose my beliefs on anyone, I personally don't support trophy hunting or the idea of ending an animal's life for the sole purpose of it becoming a decoration in mine or anyone's home.

What I do understand is that millions of animals die every single day (quite possibly trillions, if you count insects) of natural causes or by means that don't include game hunting. If there is a possibility of preserving some of those specimens, I'm all for it.

I fully understand and respect that some do not approve of taxidermy under any circumstances, or just don't wish to have real, preserved animals in their homes. It is for that very reason that I have always provided a vegan option to every project featured on *Gothic Homemaking* that involved taxidermy, skeletons, and the like.

Having said all of that, I have several stuffed ravens and crows in the Lair of Voltaire that were legally and ethically sourced and they are undoubtedly my favorite corvid-related pieces.

A Touch of the Grotesque

Scan the highest parts of any medieval castle or cathedral and you're likely to see some ghoulish faces staring back at you: gargoyles. It's believed that these waterspouts were intentionally carved as hideous beasts to ward off evil spirits.

Affordable Styrofoam gargoyles can typically be found around Halloween but might need a bit of work to look convincing (see page 66 for tips and tricks). I personally prefer stone gargoyles, though their heaviness might limit just how big of a baddie you can get into your crypt. Resin gargoyles are a lightweight and realistic option.

The Walls Will Crawl

A good place to start your lair's transformation is with your walls. The most obvious solution is to paint all your walls black. I've seen it done with some success, but I feel that painting all the walls in a room black can make the place look smaller and darker.

If your room is quite large, that might not be a concern. And if you plan to light the place with neon signs and colored strip lighting, creating a 24/7 vampire love den, go for it! My apartment is too small, so what I've done instead—and what I highly recommend you try—is paint one black accent wall. That way, you state your commitment to the Gothic lifestyle without painting yourself into a tiny dark box.

Use a black accent wall to add a touch of the macabre, or go full black-on-black for your color palette!

The Painting of (Dorian) Gray

If black is too much for you, gray is an excellent option. It offers versatility, as there are hundreds of shades of gray paint on the market. When choosing a gray paint, consider how cool or warm you want the shade to be, and always paint a sample on the wall to make sure it dries to your desired shade. I tend to like cool grays more than warm grays, so I originally chose one with a bit of blue in it. The paint looked fine on the paint chip. It even looked fine in the can. But when it dried, it was *lavender*!

Needless to say, I repainted the Lair with a warmer gray.

Stuck on Stickers

Gray walls can be a nice, neutral surface to build on, but they might not exactly scream *Gothic*. Something you can do to change that is to use vinyl wall decals (like I did in *Gothic Homemaking*, episode three, "A Shame of Thrones Part 1"). They come in many shapes, themes, and sizes, with some big enough to cover an entire wall.

For the Lair, I used a variety of designs, including barren tree branches, crows, and chandeliers. And since they are all black, they really pop on the light-gray walls. If you choose to paint your walls a dark gray or black, white decals are a great choice—you always want to choose a bold opposite to stand out. I have seen white decals on dark gray walls for a combination that looks not only macabre, but also really elegant and stylish.

Vinyl wall decals are also removable, so if you tire of the motifs you've selected, you can take them down by heating them up a little with a hair dryer and peeling them off the wall.

White Room

Believe it or not, an all-white color scheme can be extremely Gothic. A perfect place to start is to add Baroque filigree to the walls and ceiling. Then paint all the surfaces white. Next, buy Gothic thrones and other furniture in white. Make note that the style of furniture companies often describe as Gothic is actually Baroque. Pick an elegant white chaise with elaborate Baroque woodwork in a glossy white and place it in the center of this white room on top of a shaggy area rug. Hang lace curtains on the windows and maybe even over some of the furniture. Add a white chandelier, some white candelabras, and *lots* of white candles. Add some gargoyles and perhaps a faux deer taxidermy painted white on the wall, and you will swear an otherwise traditional Gothic room died and came back as a ghost!

Color Me Gothic

Monochromatic palettes are not the only choices you have when painting your lair. There are many color schemes that work wonderfully and can still be quite macabre.

Vinyl wall decals are a cost-effective and renter-friendly way to add elegance to your lair when painting the walls isn't an option.

 **Black and Red:** These colors summon up the sultry lair of a sexy creature of the night, particularly when you use lots of ornate red fabrics, like velvet, silk brocade, and other lush materials. It's best when the Gothic (again, Baroque) furniture has rich red upholstery and black lacquered woodwork. Add some ornate mirrors (even though you cast no reflection!) and perhaps a framed portrait of Vlad the Impaler. Gold accents take this color scheme from sanguine sultriness to Eastern European vampire royalty.

 Black and purple: This is the color scheme that I chose for the Lair. Purple is a regal color, perfect for a space worthy of darkside royalty. In the end, the color scheme really ended up being black, gray, and purple, with pewter being the tone of all metal surfaces. If anything, it proved that you can really personalize your space using the colors *you* love to make your home not just Gothic, but, more importantly, a place that represents *you*.

 **Black, white, and green:** These colors together might bring to mind a certain poltergeist whose name you should never say three times. Black and white stripes can look great, and with a dash of green, in the form of spooky throw pillows or some glowing uranium glass, it might just be "showtime!" Also consider adding plants—rather than furniture or paint—to bring in the green.

 **Black and gold:** Another elegant color scheme is black and gold. Add off-white as an accent color for greater visual interest without taking away from the overall feel. Picture an off-white human skull wearing a gold crown sitting on a stack of black leather books and you'll have an idea of where I'm going with this.

 **Black and pink:** Gothic Barbie? Why not? A couple of Halloweens ago, Michaels launched a line of Halloween home decor that was black and pastel pink and that raised more than a few eyebrows. But the color scheme sold so well that it stuck around and even spread to other stores. If this proves anything it's that no matter what colors you have in mind, you can make them work in a Gothic home.

Black and orange: This color scheme is a classic, *the* Halloween theme! Add off-white as an accent color and fill your home with jack-o'-lanterns, ghosts, bats, and spiders. For those who prefer to decorate for Halloween closer to October 31st—say, around midsummer—we'll get more into this color scheme in the Halloween section.

Black, red, and sepia: At one point in the Lair, I'd painted all the walls a blood red, all the furniture was black, and the rest of the items in the Lair were wooden crates, old, weathered treasure maps, and other objects in sepia tones. The result was an old-timey space with a Gothic edge that seemed almost as piratey as it was vampiric. (There I go again with the vampirates!) Use what you like from Gothic and dark decor aesthetics and add your own flavor to create a home that reflects you.

Black and white: I saved this one for last for a reason. While perfectly good for creating a sleek Gothic abode, it tends to be the default scheme for those who are not allowed to paint their walls. Speaking of which . . .

Renter's Lament

I receive many messages from viewers of *Gothic Homemaking* telling me that they are not allowed to paint the walls of their home, often because they are renting. The good news is that if your walls are white, you have a perfectly good backdrop to work with.

I suggest you focus on adding interesting black furniture and decorations to create a sleek Gothic lair. While most Gothic spaces tend to be maximalist, maybe this is the time to try a more minimalist approach. If you are not allowed to hang anything on the walls, black bookshelves or a black cabinet can be placed against those walls to cover up some of the empty white void. Place a tall, black, wooden table against the wall and top with a large cathedral-arch mirror, leaned against the wall, to cover up more of the white space.

I also suggest adding an accent color. Source a few objects that are red or silver (or whatever color speaks to you) to add a bit of dimension. Treat the space like an art gallery of spooky things.

This might also be the time to see if vinyl wall decals really *do* come off without damaging the walls. Don't think of the white wall as a giant eyesore but rather as a big, blank canvas to play on.

Tap. Tap. Tapestries at My Chamber Door

On a recent trip to Las Vegas, I decided to stay at the Sahara, because I'd seen some photos of rooms that appeared to have gorgeous Baroque murals on the walls. When I arrived, I was surprised to instead find that the image was printed on a large piece of fabric hung on the wall via hooks. I was impressed by the ingenuity. I then realized that I could hang tapestries on a wall of the Lair and switch them out whenever the mood struck.

As for where to find tapestries big enough for your wall, I'd suggest Society 6. There are many Gothic artists on there, myself included, offering some of their art in the form of tapestries. You might just find something creepy enough to transform that boring white wall into a real dreamscape of darkness. If you can't put nails or hooks in your walls, consider building a simple frame out of thin PVC pipes to attach your tapestries to instead.

Picture. Picture on the Wall

No paint? No problem. Create a galley wall! You just need a dozen or so framed paintings or prints.

My first suggestion would be to pick a theme and stick with it. It's easy for your galley wall to become a bit chaotic and cluttered if there isn't a central idea tying everything together. For example, my gallery wall at the Lair is a combination of original paintings and prints, but they all feature bats, crows, graveyards, or all of the above. For uniformity, I recommend buying similar frames for all the prints or sourcing some old, cheap frames from an antique shop and painting them all the same or a similar color.

If it's old photos you're after, go to an antique store and try to find photos from the same era or of the same subject matter. If one is in black and white, they should probably all be black and white. If you find an old Victorian photo of a woman in fancy dress, try to find other photos of people from the same era that have the same feel to them. The internet is your friend here, too. Anywhere online art is sold where the artist gets paid for their hard work is a good place to look.

Once you have your theme, bring in some variety. Choose both big and small pieces, to create a visually interesting display, and vary the subject matter of the art and in the treatment of the frames just enough so it doesn't all look too planned out.

Weird Wallpaper

Wallpaper is a fantastic way to transform your walls into the kind you might find in a real haunted home. Many people creating Gothic lairs tend to choose damask patterns; black velvet repeating pattern on a black or red paper background.

When I was first transforming my creepy kitchen, I used a peel-and-stick wallpaper that I found on Spoonflower that featured skulls and tentacles. The wallpaper from Spoonflower comes in a traditional version, which requires you add wallpaper paste, as well as peel-and-stick. I have to admit that I was skeptical of the peel-and-stick, but it works remarkably well and when I needed to remove a panel to do some repairs on a wall, it did indeed come right off.

Now that your walls are taken care of, it's time to fill the space between them. My mission is to help you find the very best decor to make you swoon with dark delight. And that means it's time to go shopping!

This grotesque has certainly kept me safe from a few evil spirits!

5

Shopping During the Halloween Season for Year-round Decor

Walk into any Gothic lair and what is likely to take your breath away are all the amazing macabre objects you encounter between its walls. As you swirl around, mesmerized by the magically dark decor items, you might ask yourself, *Where did they find all these incredible things?* And perhaps more importantly you may wonder, *Where can I get things like this for my lair?* Wonderfully weird and decadently dark home decor items are not as hard to find as you might think. You just need to know where to look.

PREVIOUS: Pass over cartoony spiders for ones that look like they've got more bite.

RIGHT: Skip the sign for trick-or-treaters and instead choose a sign used at an actual funeral parlor!

For items like mounted insects, bones, and skulls, I look for oddities stores in places I'm traveling via a simple Google search. There are also oddities markets that pop up in various cities. I do, however, advise that when purchasing these kinds of items that you make sure the objects you are buying are ethically sourced and that they are being sold legally.

Antique shops and flea markets are another great source for creepy curios. An antique piece of furniture or lamp, with a bit of refurbishing, can be just the thing to add old-world creepy charm to your home.

You can also scour sites like Etsy for handmade objects that suit your spooky style. And since most of these objects are made by individual artisans, it's often possible to request customization to ensure they fit in with the color scheme or specific look of your lair.

There are also many macabre, Goth, and witchcraft shops across the world that specialize in Gothic fashion and dark home decor. Because these shops are usually mom-and-pop shops, they might be small and hard to find, and that's all the more reason to support them!

Some of the most reliable and consistent sources of dark decor, if perhaps unexpected ones, are big chain stores around Halloween. But be careful, or you might just end up with a crypt full of kitschy and corny bric-a-brac!

I have a philosophy I use to guide my purchases that I call "High Design versus Halloween." I avoid decorations my grandmother might have put on her front porch in October and instead choose stylish items that I can imagine encountering in an actual vampire's lair.

I recommend avoiding cheap-looking materials like plastic. Instead, I look for items that are made of natural and sustainable materials like metal, glass, ceramic, wood, or marble. They are more elegant and they are certainly better for the environment.

𝕿𝖍𝖊 𝕰𝖆𝖗𝖑𝖞 𝖂𝖔𝖗𝖒 𝕲𝖊𝖙𝖘 𝖙𝖍𝖊 𝕮𝖔𝖗𝖕𝖘𝖊

Discount home decor chains like At Home and HomeGoods start putting out their Halloween offerings as early as June! By late July, you'll find discount chains like TJ Maxx, Marshalls, and Ross have followed suit. Around late July and early August, you can expect the big craft stores like Michaels and Joann Fabrics to roll out their spooky wares. And once September comes, the more high-end home decor stores, like Pottery Barn and West Elm, will have some spectacularly spooky decor on sale. If you wait until October to go Halloween home decor hunting, all you will find are the dregs of the picked-over corpse of the Halloween season.

ABOVE: You'd need to be out of your gourd to pick a silly pumpkin when there are so many other elegant options.

LEFT: A plastic cup is fine for the little monsters but choose glass for a touch of class.

Over the years that I've been doing Halloween hauls and dark decor reviews on *Gothic Homemaking*, I've amassed quite a collection of items that give my lair a spooky flair all year long.

I will share with you a few of my favorites, in the hope that they inspire you and give you an idea of what kinds of items to keep an eye out for.

TOP LEFT: I took a bath buying this skeleton-themed drink cooler from Home Goods, but it was worth it!

ABOVE: Every salad is made so much more regal with these bat bowls from Ross.

LEFT: I have a mind to keep my kitchen utensils in this amazing metal cookie jar from Marshalls.

LEFT: I serve some morbid looks along with the snacks when I use these tombstone and skeleton hand serving dishes from Target.

BELOW LEFT: This decanter from Target was a very refreshing find!

BELOW: I keep my coins in a gorgeous metal and glass piece from Pottery Barn.

When there is an item I really want to decorate my home with that truly speaks to my personal aesthetic, but it simply doesn't exist, I make it myself! The only thing more satisfying than being able to create home decor items to enhance my Lair is being able to share them with others.

For that reason, I created the Lair of Voltaire line of spooky home decor. While I'm thrilled to make them available to all, every one of these items started as something I simply wanted to create for my own home.

TOP: I burn a lot of incense in the Lair and now I have a spooky place to do it!

ABOVE LEFT: I love those faux books that serve as storage boxes, but I couldn't find any with a realistic Gothic-horror-novel look, so I created these Treasure Tomes.

ABOVE RIGHT: Coffin-shaped wall shelves are not hard to find. But when I couldn't find any that had doors, I designed my own with crystal skull-shaped door pulls and a hand-drawn spider web motif.

ABOVE: LEFT: I wanted bats in the Lair but didn't want to risk that real ones were being killed just to become decorations. So I created these realistic Lair Bat figurines.

ABOVE: You'll find my Black Labyrinth scented candles in Forest of Shadows candle bases in just about every corner of the Lair. They add as much aromatically as they do visually.

LEFT: Even the lipstick in the Lair comes housed in a skeleton! My Cemetery Smile lipsticks are great for when you want to paint the town red (or black)!

Being able to design and make things myself has helped greatly in making a lair that is truly mine. And you can do it too! Grab your glue gun and join me in the next chapter.

Taking Your Home from Mundane to Macabre

While shopping for your haunted home is a hell of a good time, what's even more enriching is making things yourself! Nothing is more satisfying than when the peculiar pieces that adorn your den were made with your very own talons. In this chapter, I will give you some tips on how to create the items that will bring your lair to life (or is that . . . undeath?). And most of these projects are created from objects that are probably hiding in plain sight.

There is no shortage of home decor available in countless stores. But so much of it is just

PREVIOUS: Don't lose your head— you too will be able to create some of the ghoulish projects in this photo!

so . . . *mundane*. Go searching for bold, romantic, dramatic, and deliciously dark options and you'll instead find only an endless wasteland of pastels, neutrals, and earth tones that leave you feeling dissatisfied and unfulfilled. On *Gothic Homemaking*, I've taken a lot of these kinds of boring store-bought objects and transformed them into dark decor you might find in the lair of a vampire vicomte. In fact, I do it so often, I even have a name for it: I call it transforming these objects from mundane to macabre! And in this chapter, I'm going to show you just how easy it can be to take normal, everyday items and give them just the twist they need to become prized possessions in your Gothic home.

Get ready to dirty your claws and transform some horribly mundane objects into the macabre decorations your creepy crypt so richly deserves!

Before We Begin . . .

There are lots of spooky DIY projects in this book that employ many different materials and tools. Take a look at these tips and tricks before getting started.

Safety First!

DIY is exciting, but before you get started, always be sure to read any safety notices listed on your materials and tools and ensure you have the proper protective gear, like gloves, goggles, and/or aprons, and take necessary precautions. Use materials like spray paint and adhesives with the proper protective gear and either outside or in a well-ventilated room (more spray-painting tips on the next page). When a heating element is involved, whether it's an oven, a blow dryer, or a heat gun, use with caution and keep a close eye on your project to make sure everything goes according to plan.

Brushing Up

For DIY projects though, I typically use disposable chip brushes. These brushes come in various sizes, but I use the 2-inch (5 cm) brushes for most projects. They have all-natural china bristles and an all-square trim shape. The handles are solid wood, which make them easy to handle, and they can be used for most paints, stains, varnishes, acrylics, and gesso. I clean them after use whenever I can, to get the maximum amount of use out of them, but they are also inexpensive enough to toss when using with materials that are impossible or extremely difficult to clean from the brushes.

Spray Painting 101

1. Make sure the item you're about to paint is clean. Wipe it with a cloth to remove any dust.
2. Be sure to lay down newspaper or a tarp to protect the area around the object from getting paint on it. Keep in mind that spray paint can get in the air and settle several feet away, so cover at least two feet in each direction. Cover more if you're painting on a table or floor you don't want to ruin.
3. Spray paint fumes are very strong and can contain harmful chemicals, so I always recommend this be done outside. If that's not possible, paint in a well-ventilated area. Use a mask or paint respirator if painting indoors or even outdoors if you are sensitive to fumes. It's always wise to wear rubber or vinyl gloves and eye protection as well.
4. Inside the spray paint can there is a little metal ball to help mix the components of the paint. Shake the can until that ball can be heard rattling around. Once you can hear the ball inside, shake the can for a minimum of sixty seconds to ensure the paint is mixed and ready. Failing to do this can cause the paint to come out unmixed and never quite dry.
5. Hold the can about 12 inches (30 cm) away from the object you're painting and sweep horizontally across the item to create a light tack coat. This coat will make it easier for the next coats of paint to stick to the object.
6. On your subsequent coat, spray the object while sweeping across it vertically. Alternate horizontal and vertical coats, waiting for each to dry before applying the next, until the object is completely painted.
7. When spray-painting, less is more! It's best to lightly spray the object while sweeping over it rather than to apply a lot of paint directly, as the latter technique can create unsightly drips.
8. Once the object is completely covered in paint, let dry. Different spray paint brands and types have different drying times, so check the can's instructions for how long to wait before handling the object.

Gothic Bottle Candelabra

I am often asked which *Gothic Homemaking* project is the easiest. That honor goes to the Gothic Bottle Candelabra. This simple candleholder will instantly add a vampiric feel to your lair, and it requires only a short list of materials, a few steps, and such basic skills that it's the perfect way to build up your DIY confidence and start this section.

You will need:

- Two or more empty wine bottles, any size
- Matte black spray paint
- Spooky stickers, or spooky printed images and spray adhesive or a glue stick
- Candles for each wine bottle in any color you prefer

Directions:

1. Remove any existing labels from the wine bottles using warm water and soap for a cleaner finish. Dry completely, then paint the bottles with matte black spray paint. (See previous page for spray-painting tips.)
2. Once dry, add a spooky sticker and your bottles are done! Alternatively, you can print out a spooky image you feel might make for a good label, then apply adhesive to the back of the paper and press onto the bottle.
3. Add a candle to the top of each bottle.

Tip: Be sure not to use "non-drip" candles, because you are absolutely going to want a mass of cascading wax to build up on your Gothic Bottle Candelabra!

Barren Branches

Another super-easy technique I use to create a spooky Gothic atmosphere in my home is to decorate with barren branches. If you're lucky enough to have a floral district like we do in New York City, you can buy them there already painted. If you don't mind waiting for Halloween, buying them at one of the big craft stores is another option. Or, of course, you can make your own! Purchase some branches or take a walk and collect the spookiest ones you find, then use this easy technique to transform them into elevated decor.

You will need:

- Barren branches (birch or curly willow branches work best but any barren branch with a shape you find pleasing will do)
- Spray paint (in black or a color of your choice)

Directions:

1. Collect or purchase your dead, fallen branches. Remove any dried leaves or dirt, if they're from nature, then cover thoroughly with spray paint. (For spray-painting tips, see page 67.)
2. Once dry, arrange the branches in vases or attach them directly to your wall, bed's headboard, or around picture frames or other furniture.

Tip: You can experiment with matte and glossy paint finishes, to see which looks best in your space, and don't be afraid to repaint with the seasons. When Creepy Christmas comes around, you can paint the branches white or red to whip your lair into the horror-day mood.

Dead Flower Bouquet

Millions of people a year send their loved ones bouquets of red roses to show their affection. And those flowers get tossed in the trash the moment they start to wilt. What a pity! That is exactly the time to act fast to make a dead flower bouquet that will last for years and years. You can experiment with different colors of roses or different types of flowers to see which looks best in your lair. But, in my experience, white roses will make your lair look like the site of a long-forgotten funeral.

You will need:
- Bouquet of real roses
- Twine
- Hammer and nail
- Decorative ribbon of your choice

Directions:

1. Once a bouquet of roses starts to wilt, turn it upside down and tie the stems together with twine, making sure to leave two twine tails of at least 2 to 3 inches (5 to 8 cm) each after tying the knot. Tie those end pieces together to form a long loop.

2. Hammer a nail into a wall and hang the bouquet upside down from the nail via the twine loop. In a few days, the flowers will dry and become stiff, locking in their beauty.

3. Either add a decorative ribbon and leave the bouquet hanging on the wall as a decoration or remove from the wall and place the bouquet right side up in a vase. Tie a Gothic ribbon around the vase for an extra touch of beauty.

Skeleton Hand Holdbacks

Sometimes all it takes is a small detail to create a big mood. An excellent example of this is the way in which you keep your curtains open. Here's a simple technique for adding a skeletal motif to your curtain holdbacks.

You will need:

- Glue suitable for both plastic and metal (e.g., Devcon 5-Minute Epoxy)
- Two plastic, life-size skeleton hands
- Two simple black metal curtain holdbacks of your choice
- Glossy black spray paint
- Paintbrush
- Wax metallic finish in silver (e.g., Rub 'n Buff)

Directions:

1. Glue a plastic skeleton hand to a simple black metal curtain holdback. Paint the skeleton hand with black spray paint (see page 67 for tips).
2. Once dry, dry-brush silver wax metallic finish onto the skeleton hand, just barely grazing the surface, to give the holdbacks a pewter appearance.
3. Repeat steps 1 and 2 to create a second holdback.
4. Attach your skeleton holdbacks to the wall using the hardware provided and throw open your curtains to let in the moonlight!

Tip: You can also use gold, brass, copper, or whatever metallic finish would look best in your lair.

Gossamer Lace Doorway

In the Lair, there is a small kitchen as well as a hallway leading to the bathroom, neither of which have a door. I don't always want people to be able to peer into the kitchen while they are visiting, especially if it's particularly messy. I have a novel technique for covering these doorways that's super easy and adds a touch of macabre mystique! It also helps create some separation between the rooms.

You will need:

- Two ceiling hooks or nails

- One 7-foot (2-meter) lace tablecloth with Gothic motifs

Directions:

1. Attach ceiling hooks to the walls on each side of a doorway. Place them high up, near the ceiling, at the entrance of the room you wish to separate. If you don't have ceiling hooks, you can just use regular nails.

2. Grab a Gothic lace tablecloth (preferably with a spider web or bat motif) and hang it from the hook screws or nails.

Tip: One long tablecloth is usually enough to cover the whole doorway, and you can just pull it aside when you wish to cross the threshold. For a fancier approach, use two of the same lace tablecloths and install the Skeleton Hand Holdbacks on either side of the doorway to hold them open. To make the covering opaque, you can add a piece of solid-color fabric behind each of the lace tablecloths.

Macabre Art Storage Box

If your lair is anything like mine, clutter is an ever-present threat! I find it's extremely helpful to be able to hide things away in storage boxes. Here's a simple project that will allow you to create a handy storage box that is unique to your haunted home, thanks to a little decoupage.

You will need:

- An unfinished wooden box with a lid of any size and shape to suit your needs
- Acrylic paint, in black or any color of your choice
- Clippings of art you love
- Glossy decoupage glue and finisher (e.g., Mod Podge)
- Two brushes (one for paint, one for decoupage)
- Clear varnish (optional)

Directions:

1. Paint the box whatever color will best match the color scheme of your lair using the first, clean brush.
2. Clip illustrations or photographs you love from magazines or books, or print out online images.
3. Apply a coat of decoupage glue to the outside surfaces of your box with the second, clean brush and place your chosen art until the entire box is covered.
4. Once your collage is complete, brush a coat or two of the decoupage glue and finisher over the entire box. Alternatively, you can seal the box with a coat of clear varnish.

Creepy Custom Cushions

There is no shortage of creepy cushion options, especially around Halloween. But you can create a space that is uniquely yours by fashioning some cushions of your own. Choose fabrics that match your color scheme and motifs, or that really capture the aesthetic that you're going for. While some sewing is involved, this project is simple enough for just about anyone to do.

You will need:

- An existing cushion or pillow
- Spooky fabric of your choice
- Needle and coordinating color thread
- Tassels and/or embroidered patches (optional)

Directions:

1. Remove the cover from your pillow.
2. Cut two pieces of fabric that are about an inch and a half bigger than the cover. Place the two pieces of fabric together, with the back of the fabric facing outward. With needle and thread (or a sewing machine, if you have one) sew the two pieces of fabric together on three sides, leaving one side open.
3. Turn your newly stitched cover inside out and slide the pillow insert into it. Sew the remaining side shut.
4. Decorate the cover by sewing or hot-gluing tassels at the corners and/or other patches, pieces of fabric, and ribbon on the front, if desired.

Optional: You can add embroidered patches to the center of your cushion cover. A large skull, bat, medieval unicorn, griffon, or lion are some options. You can also source a large old-English embroidered letter that is the first letter of your last name or the first letter in the name of your lair and attach it to the front of the cushion to make it truly yours. Attach with hot glue if you aren't a master sewer!

Coffin-shaped Serving Tray

When ghosts (or guests) come to haunt your lair, you'll want to offer them some refreshments. Let them know you're dead serious about serving them by bringing the treats out on a coffin-shaped serving tray.

You will need:

- Three or four pieces of ¼-inch (6 mm) thick coffin-shaped wood
- Wood glue
- Clamps
- Black lacquer spray paint
- Clear varnish (brush-on or spray)
- Drill
- Ornate metal drawer pulls
- Screwdriver to match screws included with drawer pulls

Directions:

1. Glue three or four identical coffin-shaped wood pieces together with wood glue. Use a clamp or two to get a good, tight bond.

2. Once dry, paint with black lacquer spray paint, then seal with a brush-on clear varnish or clear spray varnish.

3. Place drawer pulls at opposite ends of the tray as handles. Mark their positions and make the necessary holes for attaching to the tray with a drill. Screw your drawer pulls into place using the included hardware, and your coffin-shaped tray is ready to serve.

Mummified Vampire
Sumatra, Indonesia 1926

Mummified Vampire Bat Taxidermy Gaff

A taxidermy gaff is a fake piece of taxidermy made to fool someone into believing the piece was once a real, living creature. While they've been used to trick onlookers at various points in history, you can make the perfect gaff to fill a blank space in your lair. To give your gaff some extra flair, check out the Decorative Oddities Frame (on the next page).

You will need:

- A plastic bat skeleton prop
- Black acrylic paint
- Paintbrush

- A paper towel or sponge (something you don't mind getting covered in paint!)
- Thin, clear plastic sheets
- Heat gun

Directions:

1. Paint the skeleton with a liberal amount of black acrylic paint and before it dries, wipe most of it off with a paper towel or sponge.
2. Once the paint is dry, lay pieces of the plastic sheets over the skeleton.
3. To "corpse" the figure, heat the plastic sheets until they shrink and wrap around the skeleton, simulating desiccated skin.
4. Paint the bat with black acrylic paint to give it a more realistic look.

Decorative Oddities Frame

Very often, oddities are displayed in ornate frames. You can take just about any object and mount it on one of these frames to make it a beautiful point of interest in your home. You may wish to display a skull, an insect, or a piece of taxidermy, real or replica, though it does not need to be an "oddity" per se. It could be a sculpture, an old key, a doll's head, or any object you feel is worthy of display in your home!

You will need:

- An ornate picture frame
- Spray paint gloss finish (any color that works with your lair color scheme)
- Spray adhesive
- Decorative paper or fabric
- An object you wish to showcase
- Hot glue gun and glue sticks or epoxy resin
- Brass-colored corner filigree (optional)

Directions:

1. Remove the glass from an ornate frame. Spray-paint the frame to blend in better with the color scheme of your lair (or use it as is, if it already suits your style).
2. Using spray adhesive, glue a sheet of decorative paper or fabric directly onto the cardboard backing that comes with most store-bought frames.
3. You are now ready to attach your object to the board. If the object is lightweight, you can use hot glue to attach it. If the object is heavy, I'd suggest something stronger, like an epoxy resin.
4. Decorate the corners of the board with brass filigree and reattach the board to the frame.

Tip: If you're going for an old museum or cabinet of curiosities look for your piece, type out the name of the specimen in an old typewriter font and print it out on a piece of sepia-toned paper (you can make your own using the same technique found in the project Ancient Deed to Your Gothic Lair, on the next page). Cut to shape and attach to your oddities frame with glue. This will give the piece an old-world, antiquated look.

Ancient Deed to Your Gothic Lair

Pick up any old Gothic novel and you will be transported to a place where homes have stately names like Wuthering Heights, Crimson Peak, or the House of Usher. As evidenced by the Lair of Voltaire, I see no reason to wait until you own a giant mansion to experience the joy of naming your home. Moreover, whether you live in a large home or a tiny dorm room, giving your home a name not only makes you feel like it is uniquely yours, but it may also suggest what kind of decor belongs within and inspire you to decorate it further.

You will need:

- Instant coffee grounds or brown acrylic paint
- Hot water
- 2-inch (5 cm) chip brush
- A large piece of white paper
- Materials for adding text to the prepared paper (see step 2 for details)
- Lighter
- Glue or straight pins
- Decorative oddities frame (optional)

Directions:

1. Add a bit of hot water to some instant coffee grounds to create a rich, highly tinted mixture. If you prefer, you can use brown acrylic paint diluted with water instead. With a brush, paint the diluted brown liquid onto the paper. (There's no need to be neat here!) Put the wet paper out in the sun to dry.

2. Once dry, there are several ways you can add your text to the paper. You can write it yourself with a calligraphy marker, or you can hire a calligrapher. Alternatively, you can type out the text in an old Gothic font, print it out, and make or have someone make a silk screen of your text, then silk-screen the text onto the paper. Perhaps the easiest method is to print the text directly onto the aged paper using your home printer. If you choose this option, make sure your paper is no bigger than your printer will allow.

3. Once your text is transferred onto your antiqued paper, carefully burn the edges with a lighter to create an uneven border. Blow out each flame very quickly to avoid setting the whole sheet on fire!

4. Glue or attach your deed with pins to a decorative oddities frame. If you like, you can roll the paper first, so the edges stick up off the frame and give the impression that this was once an old scroll before being mounted.

Optional: To make the deed even more realistic, decorate it with an old rusty key or a wax seal. Besides the name of your lair, you might also wish to include the date on which you began to work on it and what kind of a home you wish for it to be, what kind of emotions you hope it will nurture, and perhaps which forces (spiritual, mythological, or otherwise) protect the space. And don't forget to add your signature on the bottom as the owner!

Mummified Vampire
Sumatra, Indonesia 1926

Vampire Hand Taxidermy Gaff

While we're in the mood to create things that are decrepit and old, let's try our hand at creating the severed claw of a blood-sucking ghoul!

You will need:

- Life-size plastic skeleton hand
- Heat gun (optional)
- Cotton balls
- Liquid latex
- Clear press-on fingernails
- Hot glue gun or superglue
- Sharp tool, like scissors or craft knife
- Acrylic paints in assorted colors
- A wooden dowel
- A wooden plaque
- Black acrylic paint or black wood stain
- A glass cloche

Directions:

1. Plastic skeleton hands tend to be pretty flat. If you can source one that's already in an interesting position, you are ready to begin! If not, heat a plastic skeleton hand with a heat gun until it's soft and pose the fingers into a more realistic and tortured pose. They will hold that shape once they cool.
2. Stretch cotton balls to create long strings of cotton and dip them into a cup of liquid latex. Place the latex-soaked cotton onto the skeleton hand to "corpse" the bones and create the appearance of desiccated flesh.
3. Add fake fingernails to the tips of the fingers with hot glue or superglue. Use a sharp tool to create cuts in the fingernails and make them look weathered and old. Add more latex-soaked cotton around the nails to create cuticles, so the nails appear to be growing from under the skin.
4. Once dry, paint the hand with acrylic paints to look like desiccated flesh.
5. Paint a wooden dowel and a wooden plaque with black paint or wood stain. Once they're dry, glue the desiccated vampire hand to the wooden dowel so the hand is standing up at the end of the stick, and then glue the dowel to the wooden plaque.
6. Display your morbid trophy under a glass cloche.

Creepy Candle Clusters

Nothing says "You've entered a Gothic home" quite like a mass of burning candles! Unfortunately, with that much open flame comes the danger of sending the whole place up in flames. For that reason, it might be a good idea to have some flameless candles on hand to illuminate your lair instead.

You will need:

- Several pieces of PVC pipe, at least 1½ inches (3.8 cm) in diameter
- A PVC pipe cutter
- Dremel tool with a grinder attachment
- Wire mesh
- Hot glue gun and glue sticks or epoxy resin
- Heat gun
- Wooden plaque
- Matte spray paint in your chosen color
- Battery-operated flameless tea lights

Directions:

1. Cut your PVC pipes with a PVC pipe cutter to the desired height of your "candles." I recommend cutting them to different lengths, to give the impression that some of the "candles" have burned for longer than others. While the bottoms should be cut straight so they sit flat on the base, the tops should be cut at a diagonal, to give the appearance that the "wax" has melted away.
2. Use a Dremel tool with a grinder attachment to add some variety to the shape of the top rim of the pipes, for a more natural appearance.
3. Place the bottom of one PVC pipe on a piece of wire mesh and trace the shape. Cut out a circular piece of wire mesh that is slightly larger than the pipe and use as a template to cut as many pieces as you have candles.
4. Bend the outer edges of the mesh circles upward to create small cups that will just fit into the pipes. Insert the mesh cups into the tops of each pipe and glue in place, about two inches down from the top rim.
5. Once your pipes are cut and shaped, glue them to the wooden plaque base and to each other using hot glue. (You can instead use epoxy, if you want a stronger bond.) Drip hot glue along the upper rim of the pipes and allow it to drip down the outside of the pipes, to create the illusion of dripping wax.

6. Spray-paint the entire candle cluster and base. You can use black to make creepy candles or matte white for a more traditional look. If you wish for the base to be a different color than your candles, you can either paint it ahead of time or paint it—carefully!—with a brush-on paint after attaching the candles.

7. Add battery-operated tea lights to the tops of each candle.

Gothic Birdhouse

When you look out the window of your Gothic lair, do you want to see the little birds outside living in a boring, wooden shack? Of course not! They have every right to lay their eggs in a lair as dark and regal as yours—and you can make them a spooky home of their own quite easily. Search the dollhouse aisle at your local craft or hobby store for most of these materials.

You will need:

- A wooden birdhouse, in your choice of size and style
- Polymer clay glue
- Polymer clay in various shades of gray
- Heat gun (or access to an oven)
- Terracotta-tile-textured plastic sheets for miniature model building
- Scissors
- Hot glue gun and glue sticks
- Acrylic paint in black, white, and gray
- Sponge
- A wooden base that fits your chosen birdhouse
- High-density blue Styrofoam
- A rasp for shaping the foam
- Miniature tombstones, creepy trees, gargoyles, and dollhouse finials
- Black metal chain (optional, for hanging the birdhouse)

Directions:

1. Apply a thin layer of polymer clay glue to the sides of the birdhouse. Roll the polymer clay into small balls of varying sizes and press them onto the walls of the birdhouse to simulate stones.
2. Bake the polymer clay with a heat gun. Alternatively, you can put the whole birdhouse in the oven at 200°F (93°C, gas mark 1) until the clay is baked. Monitor frequently so as not to burn down the house. (I mean the one for the birds, but that goes double for your own!)
3. Cut the terracotta-textured plastic sheets to size and glue to each side of the roof with contact cement.
4. Paint the house black. While the paint is still wet, wipe the excess paint off the stones. Sponge a lighter gray paint over the stones to create more dimension.
5. Place the birdhouse onto the wooden base and trace the shape of the house onto the wood with a pencil. Cut a piece of blue Styrofoam to fit on the base on either side of the spot reserved for the house and glue to the top of the base with hot glue.

6. Use a rasp to shape the blue foam into a hilly landscape. Arrange some store-bought miniature tombstones (or ones made of baked polymer clay, if you're feeling creative!) on the blue foam landscape and carve slots for them to sit in.

7. Remove the tombstones and paint the landscape with black paint. Dry-brush gray acrylic paint onto the landscape, then attach your tombstones, creepy trees, and gargoyles. You can also create some stone pillars using polymer clay.

8. Add dollhouse finials to the roof and around the house to look like a wrought-iron fence. If you want to hang the birdhouse, add a black metal chain to the roof.

Optional: For a much simpler version of the Gothic birdhouse, simply paint the wooden birdhouse with black paint and decorate with creepy or alchemic symbols using a white paint marker.

Gothic Lamp Transformation

On *Gothic Homemaking*, I created a Gothic table lamp called the Bordello Bones Table Lamp using some more elaborate techniques. But truth be told, you can transform just about any lamp from the mundane to the macabre using a simplified version of that tutorial.

You will need:

- Table lamp and lampshade of your choice
- Glossy black spray paint
- Disposable chip brush
- Wax metallic finish (e.g., Rub 'n Buff) in color of your choice
- Paper (for creating a template)
- Gothic fabric of your choice, enough to cover your chosen lampshade
- Spray adhesive or contact cement
- Plastic sheets or pieces of garbage bags large enough to cover the lampshade (optional)
- Hot glue gun and glue sticks
- Ornate ribbon
- Tassels

Directions:

1. Start with a table lamp, either new or antique, and remove the shade. Paint the body of the lamp with black spray paint (see page 67 for tips). Once the paint dries, dry-brush your chosen wax metallic finish over the paint.

2. Trace the shape of each side of the lampshade with a piece of paper to create a template. Place the paper template on an ornate or spooky fabric and cut out enough pieces to cover the shade.

3. With spray adhesive or contact cement, glue the new fabric to the sides of the original shade. If using spray adhesive, be sure to cover the pieces that have already been glued with plastic sheets or pieces of garbage bags to protect them from glue splatter. Once all sides of the shade have been covered in your new, spooky fabric, use hot glue to attach ornate ribbon along the vertical ribs and the top and bottom of the shade. Glue tassels at the ends of each of the shade's vertical ribs.

Optional: If you want to take this project to a new level, consider attaching a spooky object—a creepy doll, some artificial vines, or a large plastic skeleton hand, for example—to the body of the lamp before painting it. Attach your oddity to the lamp with some thin, black annealed wire and glue into place with epoxy resin. Once painted, the creepy object will appear to be part of the body of the lamp. For a Dark Academia look, consider using a worn, green oxidized finish instead of a weathered, metallic one.

The Haunted Library End Table

As functional as it is phantasmagorical, this small table is the ideal place to put a bowl of candy for trick-or-treaters, or upon which to pen that horror novel you've been working on. It's also a highly customizable piece of furniture, which can be created to suit any space, in terms of size and color.

You will need:

- Miter box
- Handsaw
- ¾-inch (1.9 cm) wide ornate wood trim
- Two pieces of 13 x 13 x ¾-inch (33 x 33 x 1.9 cm) plywood
- Hot glue gun and glue sticks or wood glue
- Brush-on enamel paint in your preferred color and finish
- Two 1-inch (2.5 cm) threaded metal floor flanges
- Screws
- One 24-inch (60 cm) threaded black steel pipe
- Four resin skulls
- Drill with 1-inch (2.5 cm) paddle bit or hole saw
- About eight faux-book storage boxes of varying sizes
- 13 x 13-inch (33 x 33 cm) ornate picture frame
- A Ouija board
- Clear varnish

Directions:

1. Using a miter box and saw, cut the ornate wood trim to fit the sides of one of the plywood pieces and glue the trim to the plywood using hot glue or wood glue. This piece will be the base of the table.
2. Paint the plywood base. Once dry, attach one of the metal floor flanges to the center of the plywood base with screws. Screw the black steel pipe into the floor flange. You now have a wooden base with a metal pipe jutting up from it.
3. Hot glue the four resin skulls to the wooden plywood base, facing away from the pipe. (You can use epoxy for a stronger bond.)
4. Drill a 1-inch hole in the center of all your faux-book storage boxes with the paddle bit or hole saw attachment on your drill. Thread your faux books onto the metal pipe. It's best to start with the biggest at the base and then work your way up to the smallest.
5. Screw the second metal floor flange to the bottom of the second plywood piece. We'll call this piece our tabletop.
6. Glue the Ouija board to the top of the tabletop with hot glue, then glue your custom-made frame to the top of the tabletop. Seal with clear varnish.
7. Screw the framed tabletop onto the end of the metal pipe and place in your lair.

Apothe-scary Cabinet

I've saved this piece for last as it was one of the most ambitious projects I've created on *Gothic Homemaking*. Perhaps because of that, it's also one of the most impressive!

You will need:

- A wooden medicine cabinet with shelves and doors that have glass panes, your choice of size and style
- Black gloss enamel paint
- Medium grade 60-100 grit sandpaper
- ⅛-inch (3 mm) black foam core board
- One roll of spooky peel-and-stick wallpaper
- Brush
- Silver wax metallic finish (e.g., Rub 'n Buff)
- Silver permanent marker
- Two X-ray images of your choice
- Two metal skull-shaped door pulls
- Two miniature plastic skulls

Directions:

1. Remove the doors, glass, shelves, and all hardware from the medicine cabinet. Paint all wooden surfaces with black gloss enamel paint. Once the paint is dry, lightly sand it to give it a distressed appearance.
2. Measure the inside back wall of the cabinet and cut a piece of foam core to that size. Cut a piece of wallpaper that matches the size of the foam core, remove the backing, and stick to the foam core. Insert the new backboard into the cabinet and put the shelves back in.
3. Dry-brush silver wax metallic finish on the doors and on the edges of the cabinet to give these surfaces a metallic appearance. Draw a spider web motif with a silver marker at the upper corners of the doors.
4. Trim two X-rays to fit in the window of each of the doors. Reattach the glass with the X-rays behind them to the doors.
5. Replace the knobs that came with the cabinet with metal skull-shaped door pulls.
6. Paint two miniature plastic skulls with the silver wax metallic finish and glue them to the top of the cabinet as a decorative element.

Optional: For an extra fancy touch, if your cabinet has a shelf above or below the doors, add some decorative stained-glass spider webs to the corners. When hanging the finished product, due to the heaviness of the cabinet and the items you'll be filling it with, it's imperative to ensure you screw it into a wood stud in your wall. I'd suggest two screws, one near the top of the cabinet and one near the bottom. If it's not possible to secure the cabinet stud, consider placing the cabinet on a high table or a bookshelf.

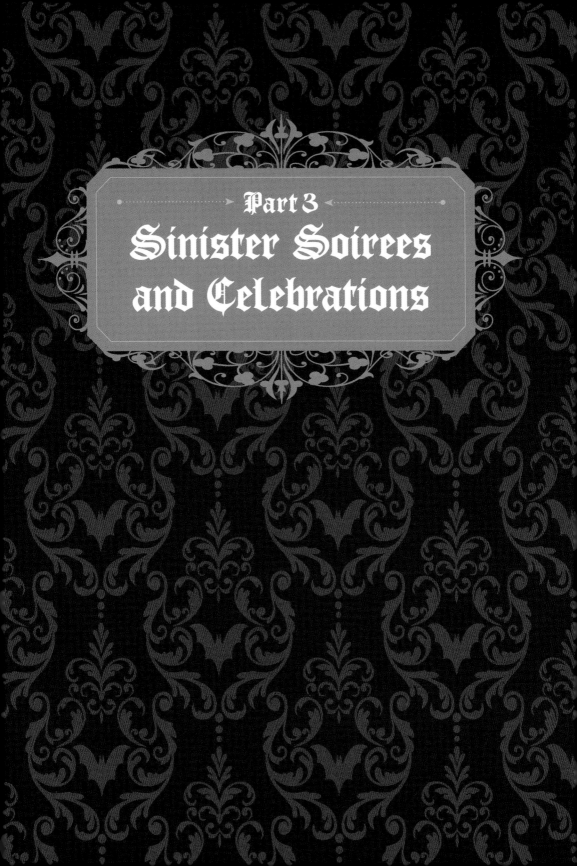

Part 3
Sinister Soirees
and Celebrations

7

Entertaining the Creatures of the Night

After decorating your home-sweet-haunted-home, it's time to invite like-minded souls over for a macabre meal, creepy cocktails, or a spooky spot of tea. By now, your lair is surely decked in dark decor, so all we really need to do to prepare for your Gothic dinner party is find the right decorations and atmosphere.

Your Spooky Tablescape

First, decide on a color scheme. Black on black is perhaps the most obvious choice, and it's a great one at that, but as I pointed out on pages 51-53, it's certainly not your only option. This is *your* party, so pick the color scheme that best reflects who you are or what kind of mood you want to set.

Here are the effects you'll get from some of my favorite color schemes:

 Black on black: Deathly serious. You are dark and you mean business! It doesn't get any more Gothic than this.

 Black and red: Sexy, romantic, vampiric

 Black and purple: Rich and regal

 Black, purple, and green bring to life a Disney villain theme

And **black, white, and green** might just summon Beetlejuice!

Once you've chosen a color scheme, it's time to pick a tablecloth. Choose cotton, velvet, or other natural fabrics. Lace is also a great option, especially when layered over a solid color to add interest and texture.

You can also use a patterned tablecloth. Spider webs, skulls, and bats are always welcome images on a Gothic dining room table. I have purchased some really lovely ones with these motifs over the years at places like HomeGoods and Pottery Barn.

Next, you'll need some placemats. A cloth placement in a solid color like black, gray, white, purple, or red is always a simple and fine way to start, or, like with tablecloths, you can opt for patterns or illustrations. There are some great Gothic ones on Spoonflower and Society 6 (including a few of my own designs). As a general rule, if the tablecloth has a design, the placemats should be a solid color, and vice versa, otherwise the table might start to look too busy.

After placemats, napkins. Black paper napkins will do in a pinch, but cloth ones will elevate your affair. If you can find napkins with Gothic motifs, even better!

You can really have some fun with napkin rings, too. I've seen some on Etsy shaped like bats, and during Halloween you can find napkin

rings with spider web, bat, or skeleton motifs. In recent years, I've seen many metal napkin rings shaped like a skeletal hand. I love these so much that I always buy a set or two, despite already owning several. At this point, I have more skeleton-hand napkin rings than I have friends!

With all our linens in place, it's time for tableware! I bought a set in black for four at Kmart over a decade ago that included dinner plates, salad plates, bowls, and mugs, all for around twenty dollars, and I still use it. Your tableware set does not have to be expensive to be perfect for you.

Also keep in mind that while some foods might look great on a black plate (like mashed yams!), some disappear against the darkness (like black foods, for instance, which I'll get to later in this chapter). When you're entertaining, you want the food you prepare to look both appetizing and amazing. For this reason, I suggest white plates with a wonderfully macabre motif. Choose glass or metal for a more elegant feel.

There are also some great flatware options on the market that come in a black finish. But keep in mind your tablecloth choice—black forks might be tough to find on a black background! In that case, opt for a silver or gold tone. Any flatware set with an elegant and baroque pattern is a fine choice, but I have a soft spot for skeletal cutlery!
I periodically scour eBay and Amazon for flatware with just such a motif and I sometimes get lucky when I roll the bones. Over the years, I've amassed several skeletal flatware sets, as well as skeleton-themed butter knives, cheese spreaders, salad tongs, and more!

PREVIOUS: Take your seat! We're having some friends for dinner.

ABOVE: A hauntingly handsome example of the black-on-black place setting.

Next, we source our glassware. I have glassware that features a small metal skeleton holding up a wineglass or martini glass, and glasses that feature a metal skeleton hand wrapped around the clear glass (with matching decanter). I have a collection of champagne flutes in both black and clear glass with a metal skeletal hand motif. There are also goblets and wine glasses out there in black or red glass that will make your guests feel like vampire royalty.

Setting the Mood

If your lights are on a dimmer, bring them down. If they are not, I'd suggest turning off your main overhead lights and using smaller floor or tabletop lamps instead. Drape lace or other translucent fabrics over the lamps to give the room a mysterious glow. Nothing is more romantic than a candlelit dinner, so bring out those candelabras for the feast.

We're not afraid of patterns and colors in this Lair!

Light some incense in a coffin-shaped incense burner to fill the room with an intoxicating, witchy scent. I personally like palo santo or sandalwood, but you should burn the scent that most excites and speaks to you. Be sure to ask your guests how they feel about incense first, though! People with respiratory issues or sensitivity to smoke or strong smells might find incense distressing. The idea is to delight your guests, not to send them screaming and wheezing into the night.

And then, what to play during a Gothic dinner party? If your guests are fans of

Gothic rock, it's hard to go wrong with a playlist of the classics, though don't hesitate to give some new bands a spin! Another great option is dark classical music. Pieces like "Danse Macabre" by Saint-Saëns, "Lacrimosa" or "Requiem in D Minor" by Mozart, or "Carmina Burana" by Carl Orff will transport your party to a dark castle in a black forest.

What's Your Pleasure?

When it comes to food and drink, choose *quality over kitsch*! Wine bottles with horror-themed labels might look great on that spooky table of yours, but things will go sour fast if what's inside is not just horror-themed but actually . . . *horrible*. A good plan is to pick up bottles of the wines you plan to serve a few days before the party and taste them to weed out the real monsters.

When planning your meal, it's extremely important that your guests enjoy a delicious and well-prepared meal made with fresh, quality ingredients. If you can make that meal look macabre, go for it! But the aesthetics of the meal should never outrank the quality of the food.

When crafting recipes, I like to imagine what might be served in, to quote *The Rocky Horror Picture Show*, "a hunting lodge for rich weirdos," or what kind of meal might have been served by candlelight while visiting Lord Byron or Percy and Mary Shelley.

Now that the scene is set, it's time to create decorations and plan your menu!

Pick your poison from one of these delicious bottles.

Safety First

Read all safety notices on your materials and tools and ensure you have the proper protective gear before getting started. See page 66 for other helpful reminders and tips.

Bat's Wishes Place Card

Place cards are a devilishly easy way to make every ghoul who walks through your door feel right at home. They also have the added benefit of making your ordinary kitchen table into an elegant place to dine. Thankfully, you don't have to pay a fortune to make something eye-catching and Gothic.

You will need:

- Small, barren, dried branches (birch is preferred if using natural, though artificial branches also work)
- Black spray paint (matte, satin, or glossy depending on your personal preference)
- A small vase
- Small rocks or pebbles to weigh down the vase, or plaster of Paris
- A heat gun
- Small plastic skeleton
- Hot glue gun and glue sticks
- Pencil
- Black construction paper
- Scissors
- White paint marker or metallic marker

Directions:

1. Gather some small, dried branches and paint them with black spray paint (see page 67 for tips). If you can't find real branches, artificial ones will do.
2. Fill the bottom third of a small glass vase with pebbles to weigh it down. Alternatively, mix up a small batch of plaster of Paris and pour that into the vase until it fills the bottom fourth.
3. Insert the branches into the vase, trimming them until they stick out about 9 inches (23 cm) above the rim of the vase.
4. Use a heat gun to pose the arms of the skeleton into a holding position. Glue the skeleton to the side of the vase with hot glue.
5. Sketch or trace a bat shape onto a piece of construction paper with a pencil and cut out the bat. With a white paint marker or metallic marker, write the name of your guest across the body of the bat, then glue the bat into the skeleton's hands with hot glue.

Bloom and Doom Centerpiece

Who doesn't love flowers? Especially when they're dead! This stunning centerpiece will capture the attention of every guest, while also allowing you to make use of any random bones that haven't yet found a home in your lair.

You will need:

- A large, oval-shaped serving tray
- A cake stand
- Spray paint, any color and finish (optional)
- A block of floral foam, sized to fit on the cake stand
- Dried or artificial flowers of your choice

- Dried, barren branches of your choice
- Hot glue gun and glue sticks
- Dried moss
- Two replica human skulls
- Bones of assorted shapes and sizes
- Black-painted pine cones, dried flower petals, or other natural decorations of your choice (optional)

Instructions:

1. Find an oval-shaped serving tray that will fit nicely at the center of your table and a cake stand that will fit well on the tray. If desired, spray-paint each of the objects to match your color scheme.
2. Once dry, place the serving tray at the center of your table. Next, place the cake stand in the center of the tray.
3. Place the block of floral foam on the cake stand. Cut the stems of the dried or artificial flowers to size, then stick them into the foam block to create a bouquet. Add some wispy barren branches to the bouquet for height and added creepiness.
4. Hot glue moss to the sides of the floral foam to disguise it.
5. Place the replica skulls on the tray beneath the cake stand, facing different directions so they can keep an eye on your guests. Add small bones on the tray around the skulls. You can also add other dried flora to give the impression of a forest floor.

Tip: Spray paint has a very strong odor that takes a few days to truly dissipate, so paint your pieces a week ahead of your dinner party so your aromatic meal isn't competing with that chemical smell.

The Bloodbath

Yield: 1 drink

Cocktails present countless color and flavor options to fit your feast to perfection. There is a cocktail that is so ubiquitous in my neck of the Gothic woods that it might as well be the official cocktail of the New York City Goth and vampire scene: the Bloodbath. It's delicious and decadent and deceptively easy to concoct.

Ingredients:

- 5 ounces (148 ml) red wine
- 1 ounce (30 ml) Chambord
- Splash of cranberry juice

Directions:

1. Pour red wine into a wine glass. Add the Chambord and a splash of cranberry juice. Stir and serve.

➤ Fear Royale ◄

Yield: 1 drink

I happen to be a big fan of champagne cocktails. I'm known to enjoy a Kir Royale—
that's a deliciously dark drink made from champagne and crème de cassis, a
blackcurrant liqueur—at brunch now and again. I also have a bottle of blackcurrant
whiskey called Von Payne that comes in the most Gothic bottle I've ever seen. The
whiskey pours out of the mouth of a gargoyle at the top of the bottle! So how about a
creepy champagne cocktail inspired by the Kir Royale?

Ingredients:

- 5 ounces (148 ml) champagne, chilled
- 1 ounce (30 ml) Von Payne
  blackcurrant whiskey
- One or three Luxardo maraschino
  cherries to garnish

Directions:

1. Pour the chilled champagne into a flute. Add the whiskey. Garnish with a cherry
   (or three) and serve.

𝕭𝖑𝖔𝖔𝖉 𝕭𝖊𝖗𝖗𝖞 𝕻𝖚𝖓𝖈𝖍

Yield: 8–10 servings

If you'd rather spend your evening playing the elegant and mysterious vampire host instead of Renfield the bartender, mix up this simple and deliciously dark punch sure to please a crowd of even the thirstiest dinner guests!

Ingredients:

- 3 cups (720 ml) cranberry juice
- 2 cups (480 ml) blackcurrant juice
- 2 cups (480 ml) cherry juice
- 1 cup (250 ml) pineapple juice
- 4 cups (950 ml) ginger ale (regular or diet)
- Juice of 1 large lime
- 10 whole cloves
- 10 whole allspice berries
- Sparkling water (optional)
- ½ cup (76 g) fresh raspberries
- ½ cup (76 g) fresh blueberries

Directions:

1. In a large punch bowl, combine the cranberry juice, blackcurrant juice, cherry juice, and pineapple juice.
2. Add the ginger ale and the lime juice.
3. Place the whole cloves and whole allspice berries in a tea diffuser and drop it into the punch. Let the punch sit in the refrigerator overnight.
4. Just before serving, taste the mixture and add sparkling water to dilute to taste, if desired.
5. Add the raspberries and blueberries and serve.

Optional: Don't forget to set up some dry ice around the punch bowl to really wow your guests! But remember: use caution when handling dry ice and do not ingest it.

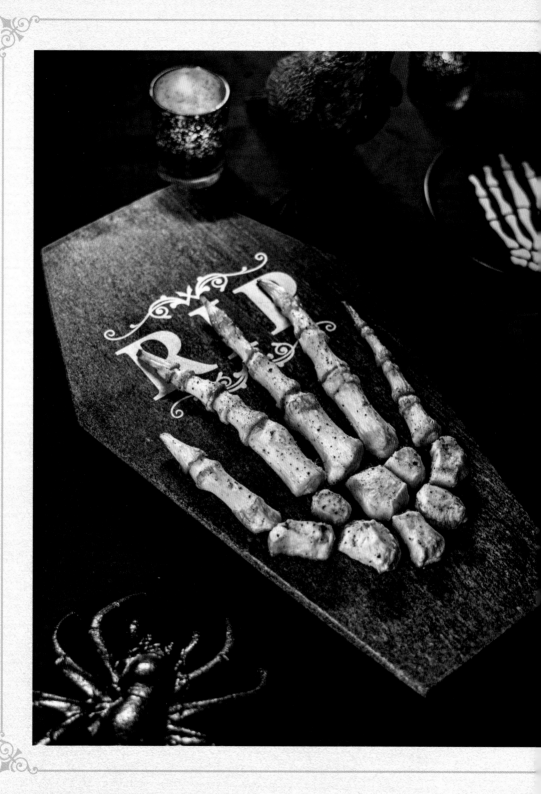

Roasted Skeleton Hand

Yield: 4–6 servings

Skeletons aren't just spooky-scary—they can also be delicious! Parsnips are an excellent autumnal treat, meaning they're a perfect fit for your Halloween-loving crowd.

Ingredients:

- 6 parsnips (5 long and thin, 1 short and thick)
- 3 Tbsp olive oil
- Salt and pepper

Directions:

1. Preheat the oven to 400°F (200°C, gas mark 6). Place a shallow metal roasting pan in the oven to heat.
2. Lightly peel the long and thin parsnips with a vegetable peeler. Cut the parsnips into smaller pieces that simulate the bones in human fingers. You can shape the pieces to more closely resemble bones, if desired.
3. Cut the short and thick parsnip into a few round slices that are about ½-inch (6 mm) thick. Using an illustration of a skeleton hand as a guide, cut pieces from the parsnip slices to simulate the bones in the palm of a human hand.
4. Put all parsnip pieces in a large bowl. Add olive oil and salt and pepper to taste. Toss until the pieces are coated with oil and spices.
5. Lay the parsnip pieces onto the roasting pan and return to the oven. Cook for 20 minutes, checking periodically to ensure they don't burn.
6. Arrange the pieces on a plate to simulate a skeletal human hand.

A Culinary Celebration of the Color Black

As we've explored, nothing says Gothic quite like the color black. As it happens, there are some foods out there that come in this foreboding shade.

Squid ink linguini: This dried black pasta comes ready to cook. Just drop it in some boiling water and a few minutes later, you've got a mass of what looks like long black worms on your nice white skeletal plate. Add a dollop of cuttlefish ink—a super thick black paste—to your favorite pasta sauce recipe and your guests will swear you've summoned this delicious, black, tentacled mass of a dish straight from the dark depths of the underworld.

Black rice: This rice, with a nuttier and stronger flavor than white rice, is also known as purple rice or forbidden rice. At one point in history, it was forbidden for anyone other than the Emperor of China and his family to eat it. It was very difficult to grow, and so was considered a precious commodity. Black rice is also highly nutritious, so it was used in Chinese medicine and was reserved for royalty and the very powerful

"Forbidden" rice. ▼

only. Of course, since you *are* dark side royalty, I welcome you to try it! You can easily pick up a bag at Whole Foods or online.

Charcoal ice cream: Black ice cream, like many foods that are artificially tinted black, gets its color from activated charcoal. Activated charcoal is a fine, odorless, black powder that is sometimes used to treat overdoses. It's said to have powerful toxin-clearing properties, so serve your guests a scoop or two after the meal and you just may be sending them home in better shape than when they arrived!

You're Going to Think I'm Buggin', But . . .

If you really want your guests to bug out, serve them insects for dinner! I first discovered the joys of eating insects while traveling through Mexico, where insects were an important part of the diet before the arrival of the Spanish. In my travels, I enjoyed black ants, deep-fried maguey worms, and more cricket and grasshopper tacos than I can count. Insects are high in protein, low in carbohydrates, and contain essential minerals including zinc, iron, calcium, and magnesium.

You can purchase edible insects that are ready to eat from various suppliers. Entosense is a company I buy from and they have a wide range of products. If you're feeling adventurous, here are some insect dish ideas:

Black ant avocado toast: Black ants have an acid in them that has a very citric taste. Sprinkle some black ants onto avocado toast and it will give the snack a bit of lemony zing.

▲ Add some crunch to your breakfast . . . with ants!

A most egg-cellent hors d'oeuvre.

Cricket salad: Crickets, like a lot of insects, just taste like whatever you cook them in. If you purchase some salted crickets, you can toss them into a salad in lieu of croutons. Unlike the ants, your guests will instantly know there are critters on their plates, so be sure to check with them first lest they start hopping right out the door before the second course!

The Devils barbed tail: Deviled eggs are delightful, but to really put them over the top, garnish each with a Manchurian scorpion! For that matter, just about any hors d'oeuvre decorated with a tasty arachnid will surely take the sting out of a dull night.

Just a big ol' bowl of worms: A fantastic conversation starter is to simply put out a big bowl of fried maguey worms. This ancient delicacy is nutritious and delicious and, yes, it's undeniably going to be weird as hell for many people. You'll know right away if your guests are squeamish or if you've found the perfect way to worm yourself right into their hearts.

While I do love a bit of shock value, I really must stress that you should gauge your guest's dietary needs and restrictions before springing something like this on them. They might be vegan or just really turned off by the idea of insects at the table. When entertaining, your only goal should be to make sure your guests feel comfortable, looked after, and respected. So, move like an inchworm if you want to venture into the realm of serving creepy crawlies to avoid your guests bugging out.

Enough Tricks—Time for Treats!

After a dark and delicious meal, you'll want to offer your guests a cup of coffee, an aperitif, or a spot of tea. Serving tea, in particular, offers the opportunity to pull out the fancy teacups and matching tea pot. There are many Gothic tea sets on the market, including some beautiful pieces by Angioletti Designs on Etsy. They make unique porcelain dinnerware and tea items that feature skulls, ravens, jewel-like green beetles, and mermaids. They also offer customization and allow you to design your own.

Killstar also has several different Gothic tea sets, including the After Midnight line, which has cups and a pot where the handles are shaped like a bat wing. Teatime is always a great time for me to pull out my collection of skeletal spoons and my Haunted Hallows jack-o'-lantern spoons by Lively Ghosts. As for what's in the teapot, my favorite tea at the moment is called Elder Goth, from Tea & Absinthe. It contains, among other things, rooibos, nettle, rosehip anise, cardamom, and, of course, clove, for that classic Goth aroma.

This tea set by Killstar is really killing it.

8

SummerWeen

At the Lair of Voltaire, we always say that every day is Halloween. And we mean it! Just because it's spring or summer doesn't mean we can't have a spooky good time. Some folks have even begun throwing halfway to Halloween, or "Halfoween," parties, on or around May 1st, to immerse themselves in the Halloween spirit.

A Halfoween party is basically a Halloween party, just during a different time of year. While others might be out soaking up the sun to celebrate the arrival of summer, we denizens of the darkness like to bring a little spookiness to the sand.

PREVIOUS: Take the tropical and make it terrifying!

Here are some tips if you're thinking of planning your own Halfoween party:

1. Keep the lights low and use string lights or any glowing novelty lights to create a spooky-yet-festive atmosphere.
2. Cover the furniture in white sheets to give your place the look of an abandoned mansion. You can also add black cloth eyes to them so the furniture all appears to be haunted by Halloween ghosties.
3. Drag that fog machine out of the garage or the attic and dust off the cobwebs! Nothing is better for creating a Halloween atmosphere than some creepy fog.
4. Just like you might during Halloween, decorate the room with cobwebs. Hang them over the light fixtures and stretch them over the mantel, the stairwell, and anywhere else they will add a creepy touch.
5. Have bowls of candy out for your guests. Don't forget the candy corn—dreaded by many, beloved by some!
6. Create a playlist of your favorite Halloween songs to transport people to October 31st, if only in spirit.
7. Make sure your guests know they must say "trick or treat" to gain entrance to your frightful affair.
8. And most importantly, make costumes mandatory!

By Midsommar, your Halfoween party will be but a distant memory . . . which is why it's the perfect time to get back in the spirit and throw a SummerWeen party! For this kind of affair, I employ a lot of the same ideas as for a Halfoween party, but I really lean into the seasonal trappings. For starters, if you have outdoor space, this might be the perfect time (and weather!) to bring the party outside. Think of the things that summer brings to mind and incorporate those themes into your decorations.

Consider throwing a terrifying tiki-themed SummerWeen party, complete with tropical drinks in tiki mugs and lawns decorated with tiki torches. There's nothing like sipping an ice-cold Zombie while discussing the latest horror films on a dark summer's night. Or throw a Skeletal Surf Safari-themed soiree with full-sized, store-bought skeletons posed in lounge chairs holding drinks or on surfboards. You can dress them like Hunter S. Thompson or the cast of *Gilligan's Island* for a chuckle. Or for a more realistic look, use the technique I outline in the Mummified Vampire Bat Gaff on page 77 to "corpse" them up, so they look like leftovers from a cannibal buffet! You can also create Styrofoam tombstones shaped like the tops of surf boards for decoration.

There is no shortage of surf music with monster themes you can use to create a playlist. Be sure to include The Cramps "Goo Goo Muck," or the original version by Ronnie Cook and the Gaylads. Other spooky surf and surf-adjacent hits include "Theme from *The Munsters*" by Jack Marshall, "Monster Beach Party" by Teen Sensations, "Hybrid Moments" by Misfits, "Riboflavin" by 45 Grave, "Zombie Hop" by Zombina and the Skeletones, "Be My Bride of Frankenstein" by Charming Disaster, "Jekyll and Hyde" by Jim Burgett, and so many others! Search for Halloween Surf Rock, Halloween Rockabilly, Halloween Ska, and Halloween Reggae to build out your own list.

▲ Birds of a bone just love the party zone.

If a skeletal surf party isn't your thing, try a vampire pool party. Encourage all your guests to wear black swimwear and sunglasses. Remind them that this is an outdoor affair and that they should dress in comfortable clothes. You wouldn't want anyone showing up in a velvet cape and frock coat! Suggest black shorts, T-shirts, the classic little black dress, or anything that will have them feeling comfortably creepy. And make sure everyone brings sunblock! I mean, it *is* a vampire pool party, after all.

Safety First

Read all safety notices on your materials and tools and ensure you have the proper protective gear before getting started. See page 66 for other helpful reminders and tips.

Gore Hole

Cornhole is a favorite North American pastime. This popular lawn game consists of two players or teams taking turns throwing bean bags made of fabric into a hole at the far end of a raised, angled board. Here's a way to transform this wholesome game into something a little darker.

You will need:

- Four store-bought organ props, such as brains and hearts
- Craft knife
- 1 pound bag of sand
- Funnel
- Hot glue gun and glue sticks
- Cornhole board
- Electric jigsaw (optional)
- Circular object, such as a metal bowl
- Medium grade 60-100 grit sandpaper
- Matte white spray paint, a brush-on latex, or enamel paint
- Red latex, enamel, or acrylic paint
- Clear varnish (optional)

Directions:

1. Cut a small hole in each organ with a craft knife and add some sand with a funnel to add weight. Seal the hole with hot glue.
2. Ensure your largest organ will fit in the hole of your cornhole board. If not, you will need to make the hole bigger with an electric jigsaw. Use a circular object like the rim of a metal bowl to mark where you will cut. Once cut, sand the edges of the hole with sandpaper.
3. Paint the cornhole board white. Once the white paint is dry, splatter red paint onto the board using a brush so it looks like blood splatter. If desired, varnish the board for a smoother finish.

Variation: For a classic Gothic version of this project, you can paint a cornhole board black and make white fabric bean bags to look like skulls. Decorate the board with white vinyl decals of bats, bones, or tombstones to create a cemetery scene. Tossing skulls into an open grave will be an absolute scream for your Gothic guests!

Creature from the Backyard Pool

This simple sea serpent prop will have your guests thinking you have *a seven-headed hydra living in your swimming pool!* Please note that this project uses Worbla, which becomes soft and malleable when heated. If you live in a high-heat area, you can use EVA foam, or consider laser-cut wood or thin plexiglass.

You will need:

- Two 20-inch (50 cm) Styrofoam life preservers
- Hand or electric saw
- Card stock or cardboard
- 24 peel-and-stick EVA foam sheets, roughly 10 x 10 x .02 inches (254 x 254 x .5 mm), in color(s) of your choice
- Six sheets of black Worbla

- Epoxy resin
- Six wooden plaques from a craft store, roughly 7 x 5 x 1 inches (18 x 13 x 2.5 cm)
- Hot glue gun and glue sticks
- Paint, in black or color of your choice
- Black metal straight bracket mending plates and screws

Directions:

1. Remove any fabric or rope from each of the lifesavers so you are left with two Styrofoam donuts.

2. Cut one of the lifesavers in half with a saw so you have two pieces, each shaped like the letter C. One piece will be the first hump of your sea serpent. Cut about 2 inches (5 cm) from the ends of the second piece. This will be the second hump of your sea serpent. For the third hump of the sea serpent, cut a C-shaped piece from the second lifesaver that's smaller than either of the first two.

3. Draw a row of tear-shaped dragon scales on a piece of card stock or cardboard. That will be row one. Draw another row of scales that fit between the scales of row one. This will be row two. Use these cardboard templates to cut enough scales out of the EVA foam sheets to cover all three humps.

4. Remove the backing and stick rows of scales along all three humps, alternating between using row 1 and row 2 scales to create a dragon skin pattern.

5. Draw a shape like a cresting wave onto a piece of card stock or cardboard. Include in your drawing a small dagger-like shape at the bottom of the spine (this will come in handy later to hold the spine in place). Use this as a template to cut out as many spines as you'll need from your sheets of Worbla.

6. Make an incision with a craft knife on the back of the first hump. Use that extra spike you drew at the bottom of the spine to anchor the spine in place. Glue with epoxy. Repeat until all three humps have dragon spines.

7. Turn two of the wooden plaques upside down and glue the ends of the first hump onto the wooden plaques with hot glue.

8. Repeat for the other two humps.

9. Paint the exposed parts of the wooden plaques, either black or the same color as the interior walls of your pool to help them camouflage better.

10. Once dry, screw a black metal straight bracket mending plate to the bottom of the wooden plaques between the first and second hump and also from the second hump to the third to hold them together.

Optional: For a more interactive sea creature, drill holes at the end of the wooden plaques and tie them together with a piece of thin black rope or black chain. Add a long piece of rope or chain to the front of the first hump's wooden plaque to use as a leash and let your guests take your sea serpent for a swim.

Vampire Vultures

Now that there's a monster in the pool, it's time to create some feathery fowl for the lawn. The most obvious Gothic choice would be to turn goofy pink flamingoes into those carrion-eating harbingers of doom known as vultures. But what if we took it a step further and transformed them into something *truly* terrifying?

You will need:

- 23-inch (58 cm) pink flamingo plastic lawn ornament
- Black satin spray paint
- Blood-red or maroon spray paint, any finish
- Hot glue gun and glue sticks
- 6-foot (1.8 meter) white feather boa
- Two sheets of 12 x 12-inch (30 x 30 cm) black EVA foam or Worbla
- One roll of ⅛-inch (3 mm) sculpture wire
- Contact cement
- Drill with ¼-inch (6 mm) drill bit
- Epoxy resin
- Brush
- Gray or white brush-on paint
- Black brush-on paint or black marker

Directions:

1. Paint the body and bottom half of the neck of your flamingo with black spray paint (see page 67 for tips). Once dry, mask off the black paint at the neck and paint the head and upper half of the neck with a dark red spray paint.

2. Add a dollop of hot glue to the neck of the bird where the black and red paint meet and attach one end of the white feather boa. Wrap the boa around the neck, adding hot glue as needed to keep in place.

3. Draw a bat wing on a sheet of foam. Cut out your bat wing with a pair of scissors. Place the bat wing on top of another sheet of EVA foam, trace it, and cut it out.

4. Cut a piece of ¼-inch (6 mm) sculpture wire and shape it on one of the bat wings to mimic where the bones would be on an actual bat wing. This wire is going to be the skeleton of the wing, allowing it to be posable. Be sure to leave at least an additional 4 inches (10 cm) of wire, for attaching the wing to the body. Use contact cement to glue the two sheets of EVA foam together, sandwiching the wire between them to create one bat wing.

5. Repeat this process to create a second bat wing.

6. Drill a ⅛-inch (3 mm) hole on either side of the plastic body. Insert the wire from each wing into the holes and epoxy the wings in place.

7. Paint the beak of your vampire vulture white or gray. Using black paint or a black marker, draw an eye on either side of the head.

𝕺ptional variation: If you prefer to make a regular vulture, either leave the wings off entirely or make black, feathery, bird-shaped wings using the same technique described above.

Watermelon Jack-o'-lantern

Since pumpkins are hard (if not impossible) to find in the summer, the watermelon is a perfect stand-in for the Halloween fixture. If you're a bit green when it comes to pumpkin carving, you might find it very refreshing to know that these are super easy to make! And don't forget to save the guts for a tasty treat.

You will need:

- One large round watermelon
- Large and small sharp knives
- A black washable marker
- A large metal spoon or scoop
- A candle or battery-operated light

Directions:

1. Cut a slice off the bottom of a round watermelon so that it sits on a flat surface without rolling away.
2. Draw a jack-o'-lantern face on the front of the watermelon with a marker. Cut the top off the watermelon so that you can access the inside, then scoop out the meat of the watermelon. Place in a clean bowl—it will come in handy as a snack!
3. Once the watermelon is empty, cut out the eyes, nose and mouth. Place a candle or battery-operated light inside and place the top back on.

ᛒlack ᛚemonade

Yield: 8–10 servings

The big, yellow, hurtful thing is in the sky and your guests are all bedecked in black. This might just be the perfect time to help them cool down! This recipe creates two liters of black lemonade for your sinister and sunny soiree.

Ingredients:

- 5 large lemons
- 2 tsp black charcoal
- 4 Tbsp maple syrup
- 2 liters water

Directions:

1. Juice 4 large lemons and pour the juice into a 3 ½-pint (1.6 L) bowl or pitcher. Add black charcoal and sweeten with maple syrup. Add water and stir.
2. Slice your final lemon to use as garnish and serve over ice.

SummerWeen Salad

Yield: 3–5 servings

I get requests for Voltaire's SummerWeen Salad all the time, so I end up making it
year-round! But it's perfect for the summer months. The sweetness of the watermelon
mixes with the tartness and saltiness of the vinegar, lime, and herbs to create a
wonderfully intriguing flavor that, like salted caramel, is both sweet and salty at the
same time. Your guests will love it!

Ingredients:

- 1 large cucumber
- 4 large vine tomatoes
- 1 ½ cups (254 g) of fresh watermelon
- Half a red onion or Spanish onion
- ¼ cup (38 g) fresh dill
- ¼ cup (38 g) fresh parsley
- Juice of 1 large lime
- 2 Tbsp extra virgin olive oil
- 1 Tbsp white vinegar
- Salt and pepper

Directions:

1. Peel the cucumber and cut lengthwise. Remove the seeds and cut into
   1-inch chunks.
2. Remove the seeds from the tomatoes and cut into 1-inch chunks.
3. Cut the watermelon into 1-inch (2.5 cm) chunks. You can use the watermelon from
   your jack-o'-lantern (page 126) or pre-cut watermelon from the supermarket.
4. Dice the onion. I use red onion because I like the nice strong flavor it has, but if
   you prefer something milder, you can use a Spanish onion.
5. Dice your fresh dill and parsley. (If you cannot find fresh herbs, *do not* substitute
   with dried. Just omit from the recipe.)
6. Add the cucumber, tomato, watermelon, onion, dill, and parsley to a large bowl,
   and then add the lime juice.
7. Add the extra virgin olive oil and white vinegar, plus salt and pepper to taste. Toss
   with salad tongs before serving.

Green Widow Spider Guacamole

Yield: 8–10 servings

Back in Chapter 7, I mentioned that when making food for your guests, one must always choose quality over kitsch. But when hosting a Halloween or SummerWeen affair, as long as you've got the quality under control, you can absolutely go cuckoo with the kitsch! I know everyone likes their guacamole a particular way, so, like everything else in this book, you should mix it up and make it your own.

Ingredients:

- 6 fresh ripe avocados
- 3 vine tomatoes
- Half a medium red onion
- ¼ cup (38 g) of fresh cilantro
- Juice of 1 large lime
- Salt and pepper
- 8 celery stalks
- 8 thin asparagus spears
- 1 red bell pepper
- 2 French green beans (haricots verts)
- 8 red sweety drop (or Peruvian) peppers

Directions:

1. Peel the avocados, remove the pits, and cut the meat into roughly 1-inch (2.5 cm) squares. Mash the avocado into a chunky paste with a pestle and mortar or with a fork in a bowl.

2. Remove the seeds from the tomatoes and cut into ½-inch (1.2 cm) squares. Dice the red onion. Roughly chop the cilantro.

3. Add the tomatoes, onion, and cilantro to the avocado and mix thoroughly, then add the lime juice. Add salt and pepper to taste and mix again.

4. Place a small piece of plastic wrap on a large, oval, kitchen spoon made of silicone or similar material and fill the spoon up with the guacamole. Scrape off the excess with a knife so the guacamole is the same shape as the spoon.

5. Turn the spoon over onto a large black plate and place the oval of guacamole onto the plate. Peel the plastic wrap off the guacamole and discard. Reshape and smooth the oval as needed. This will be the abdomen of the green spider.

6. With an ice cream scoop or melon ball scooper, grab another dollop of guacamole and deposit it in front of the abdomen so it looks like the cephalothorax of the spider (that's the part the legs come out of). Reshape and smooth as needed. Wipe away any guacamole that has spilled outside of the desired spider body shape.

7. Cut 4 pieces, each about 1 inch (2.5 cm) long, from the narrowest part of the celery sticks. Slice them lengthwise so you end up with 8 thin pieces. Those are going to act as the coxa (hip joints). Place them around the guacamole cephalothorax.

8. Cut 16 pieces of celery sticks that are 3 inches (8 cm) long. Arrange those coming out of the coxa so they make up the femurs and tibias of the 8 spider legs.

9. Cut the bottoms off the asparagus spears so the tips are just about 3 to 4 inches (8 to 10 cm) long. Boil the asparagus tips for 5 minutes. Once cooled, place the asparagus tips on the plate to form the ends of the legs.

10. Cut an hourglass shape from the skin of a red bell pepper and place it on the abdomen of your guacamole spider.

11. Cut one of the French green beans in half. Stick both pieces into the front dollop of guacamole to create the pedipalps—those are the two front pincers or appendages spiders have sticking out around their mouths.

12. Cut the second French green bean in half and stick those pieces into the back of the abdomen to create the spinnerets, the two small structures spiders have on their back ends for silk extrusion and manipulation.

13. Finally, place the peppers near the front of the smaller dollop of guacamole to create the eyes.

Tip: If you can't find sweety drop peppers, you can use salmon roe or large black peppercorns.

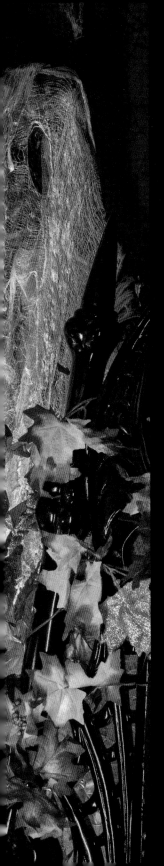

9

Halloween

When Halloween finally comes around, ghouls like us really get into the spirit! When you live a spooky lifestyle year-round, you might feel like everyone in the world is judging you for looking dark and macabre all of the time. But during the Halloween season, the rest of the world gets bitten by the boo bug. In many cultures, there is a period of time when it's believed the veil between the world of the living and the world of the dead is lifted, or is at least thinner than usual. For some, the thought that the dead can peek into our world is frightening. For those who realize that death is an inevitable part of life, it's intriguing and mesmerizing. And for those who believe that our dearly departed can visit during this time, as is the case in Mexico during their *Día de los Muertos* (Day of the Dead), it is a time to be joyful and to celebrate.

Halloween in the United States is most likely derived from Celtic harvest festivals, like the Gaelic festival of Samhain, a festival with pagan roots that marks the end of the harvest season and the beginning of the "dark" time of year. It's believed the walls between the world of the living and the Otherworld become less rigid during this time, making it possible for spirits or fairies to enter our realm. Meals would be left out to appease wandering souls, and it's believed that in time a tradition formed in which people would dress as otherworldly creatures to collect those meals. Others might collect "treats" in exchange for praying for the souls of the dead, or alternatively in exchange for a "trick," like singing, dancing, or telling jokes.

Regardless of where the traditions came from, one thing is certain: Halloween is more popular than ever!

PREVIOUS: Just when you thought the Lair of Voltaire couldn't get any spookier!

ABOVE: An arachnid acquaintance checks out our haunting Halloween decor.

In the United States, Halloween spending has increased steadily year after year and is now nipping at the heels of Christmas. According to the National Retail Federation, Americans spent $12.2 billion dollars in 2023! Considering that this spooky holiday is an opportunity to be whoever you want to be for a day while eating as much candy as seems reasonable (or even unreasonable), it's no surprise it's so popular.

As you can surely guess, Halloween is my favorite time of the year. I simply adore monsters and the macabre, skeletons and all things spooky, so Halloween is truly a gift for me. I love to decorate for this special time and make all my favorite seasonal treats. I'm excited to share some of those tips with you to help you enjoy Halloween to the fullest!

For starters, I can tell you that when it comes to decorating for Halloween, all bets are off. While I try to stick to a monochromatic palette in the Lair for the rest of the year (save bits of purple here and there), during Halloween, I dive into the traditional black and orange and all of that "high design versus Halloween" stuff goes right out the Gothic cathedral window. I replace all my throw pillows with ones in holiday-appropriate colors and choose cushions with spider and bat motifs. I bring out additional candles for a warm glow, adding orange candles to my usual black and white mix and placing them in creepy candelabras. I also break out the artificial florals in fall colors to create a large autumnal bouquet or two, and wrap garlands of orange leaves around the woodwork of my Gothic thrones and other furniture. And while I'd never do this during any other time of year, I go crazy with the spider webs! Artificial spider webs are something I would only use in decorating if I was making a haunted attraction. But during Halloween I *absolutely* want my home to look like a haunt! Which is why I'm also not opposed to putting a nice big spider in a high corner, waiting to pounce on my guests.

But believe it or not, my favorite item to decorate with during the Halloween season is the least expensive and the most environmentally friendly: pumpkins! During this time of year, you can find gorgeous gourds in many shapes and sizes. I like to add a few larger ones here and there, but honestly, it's the tiny pumpkins placed on shelves and tables and in all manner of little nooks that really complete the look.

The final touch is creating an eerie mood with appropriately creepy lighting and atmosphere. On *Gothic Homemaking*, I demonstrated "How to Create an Eerie Glow." Basically, I hide colored rope lights under and behind the furniture to cast an eerie, colorful glow onto the walls. You can also do this with LED lights. The fact that the source of the otherworldly lighting isn't seen really adds to the mystique. A low-lying mist from a well-placed smoke machine will bring it all together to create a truly haunting Halloween home.

Here are a few of my favorite Halloween DIY decor ideas to help you haunt your home, followed by some terribly tasty treats!

Safety First

Read all safety notices on your materials and tools and ensure you have the proper protective gear before getting started. See page 66 for other helpful reminders and tips.

The Classic Jack-o'-lantern

Irish folklore tells us that the tradition of making jack-o'-lanterns began with an old drunken trickster named Stingy Jack. This fellow was very crafty and was particularly fond of playing tricks on the Devil himself. When death finally caught up with Jack, he was admitted to neither heaven nor hell due to his sinful and crafty ways. The Devil gave Jack an ember to light his way through the darkness, which the man placed in a hollowed turnip to create a lantern. Cursed to wandering the countryside forever, he came to be known as Jack of the lantern, or Jack-o'-lantern. Over the centuries, the turnip was replaced with a pumpkin, creating one of the most iconic Halloween decorations.

I find that making a jack-o'-lantern is a fantastic way to get into the Halloween spirit. To make it even more festive, invite over some of your favorite ghouls for a cup of warm mulled cider (try my recipe on page 150) and the chance to create some fiendish faces!

You will need:

- A black permanent marker
- A large pumpkin
- Sharp knives or pumpkin carving tools
- A large metal spoon or scoop
- Rubbing alcohol
- A candle, real or flameless

Directions:

1. With the marker, draw a circle around the top of the pumpkin, about 3 to 4 inches (8 to 10 cm) down from the base of the stem. Use a sharp knife to cut along this circle to remove the top of the pumpkin.
2. Clean out the guts of the pumpkin. A large spoon works, but feel free to dig in with your hands! Make sure to scrape the sides to get it as clean as you can.
3. Decide which side of the pumpkin will be the front and draw a spooky face there with your marker. Use sharp knives or pumpkin carving tools to cut out your design. If any of the black marker is still visible, remove it with rubbing alcohol.
4. Insert a candle, place the top back on, and display.

Bat Cut-Outs

Here's another Halloween DIY project that is simple and yet goes a long way to setting the mood. While I would absolutely love to be able to add a swarm of *real* bats to my decor, sadly, that's just not possible. But we can create the feeling that the bats have left the bell tower and are swirling around your lair with just a bit of construction paper, some scissors, and a little creativity. Create a swarm of swirling sky puppies in no time at all!

You will need:

- 12 sheets of 12-inch x 18-inch (30 cm x 46 cm) premium heavyweight black construction paper
- Pencil
- Scissors
- Double-sided urethane foam tape
- Clear fishing line (optional)

Directions:

1. Hand draw, use a large bat-shaped cookie cutter as a stencil, or find a fitting bat shape on the internet as a template to create at least 12 bats on the construction paper
2. Cut out the bats and gently fold some of the wings, to give the illusion that they're midflight.
3. Attach the paper bats to your wall in your preferred arrangement with the urethane foam tape.
4. You can also attach the bats to clear fishing line and then attach the line to your ceiling.

Note: Though the thickness of the foam tape adds dimension, if you are concerned about the tape peeling the paint off the wall when you remove the bats, you can use masking or painter's tape instead.

Cranium Candle Holder

By now you know how much I love decorating with skulls and candles to create a wonderfully macabre mood. But you can also put these two beauties together to create a truly creepy candle holder. Holding an ornate pedestal topped with a human skull with a single white candle flickering atop it places you solidly in classic Gothic horror territory!

You will need:

- Spray paint (any color and finish, per your preference; optional)
- A small ceramic dish (roughly 1 inch [2.5 cm] deep and 3 ½ inches [9 cm] in diameter)
- One 8-inch (20 cm) tall wooden pillar candle holder
- Resin replica human skull
- Epoxy resin
- 5-inch (12 cm) coach candle (any color)
- Lighter

Directions:

1. If you'd like, spray paint the ceramic dish and wooden pillar candle holder to best match your space. Let dry fully before proceeding.
2. Glue the small ceramic dish to the top of the resin skull, then glue the skull to the top of the candle holder with epoxy resin.
3. Secure the coach candle onto the ceramic dish by melting the bottom of the candle a bit with a lighter and using the hot wax as a glue. I would suggest a white candle, but you can use any color.

𝕿ick-𝕭at-𝕮row

A Halloween party isn't all fun and games—but maybe it should be! If your guests are looking to kill some time, here is a classic pastime with a creepy spin.

You will need:

- Ten 4-inch (10 cm) heavyweight square cardboard coasters
- Black acrylic paint
- Images of bats, crows, and ticks
- Glue stick
- 12 x 12-inch (30 x 30 cm) piece of black foam core board or EVA foam
- A white paint marker

Directions:

1. Paint the front and back of the coasters. Source and print out public domain images of bats, crows, and ticks. Cut out and glue to the front of the coasters with a glue stick.
2. To create the game board, use a piece of black foam core or black EVA foam. Draw the four lines of the typical tic-tac-toe game onto the square using the white paint marker.

𝕿ip: Play this game like tic-tac-toe, but with bats and crows instead of Xs and Os. To make things even more exciting, add the image of a tick to the back of every game piece and have a six-sided die ready. Each turn, players roll the die once. If the die lands on the number 6, that player gets to turn over one of their opponent's pieces. If you expose the tick, then that piece is now wild, meaning a crow can be counted as a bat and vice versa.

Spooky Scary Skeleghosts

If you think a skull candle holder is sinister, just wait until you see some spooky scary skeleghosts hanging from the rafters! Here's a skeletal twist on the cheesecloth ghost, sure to send shivers down the spine. Two or three of these hanging from trees in your front yard will make for a phantasmagorical Halloween display.

You will need:

- A full-sized, posable plastic skeleton
- Black and brown acrylic paint
- Brush and sponge
- Hot glue gun and glue sticks
- Heat gun
- 5 feet (1.5 m) of thin, transparent plastic drop cloth
- Gray and white acrylic paint
- Three small screw-in eye bolts
- 6 feet (1.8 m) of thin framing wire
- Bucket
- White school glue (e.g., Elmer's)
- 2 yards of cheesecloth
- Tin foil
- Standard kitchen variety plastic wrap
- Gray and brown matte spray paint

Directions:

1. Separate the skeleton into top and bottom halves at the base of the spine, where it meets the pelvis. We will only be using the top half of the skeleton for this project, but I'm sure you'll find some other spooky use for the legs!

2. Paint black or brown acrylic paint onto the skeleton with a brush and wipe off with a dry sponge before the paint dries for a more realistic look.

3. Pose the skeleton with its arms reaching out. If the skeleton cannot hold the pose, glue all the arm joints to keep it in place. If the hands look too stiff, heat up the fingers with a heat gun until they are malleable and pose into a more menacing gesture.

4. Cut some pieces of the plastic drop cloth in irregular sizes and place over the arms, skull, and ribs. Heat with a heat gun until the plastic starts to melt and shrivel, to create the illusion of desiccated skin. Add layers of plastic sheeting until you're happy with the amount of "corpsing" you've created.

5. Brush some black acrylic paint over the newly corpsed skeleton and wipe off with a dry sponge before the paint dries. Gently sponge a layer of gray paint onto the skeleton with a nearly dry sponge. Once dry, sponge a lighter gray or white on top to create some highlights and dimension.

6. Once the paint on your skeleton is dry, screw an eye bolt into one of the vertebrae near the top of the spine. Loop a piece of thin framing wire through the eye bolt and use the wire to attach the skeleton to the ceiling or a clothing rack so you can create his ghastly robes.

7. In a bucket, create a mixture of two parts white school glue and one part water. Cut pieces of cheesecloth big enough to cover the skeleton's shoulder and ribs and dip into the glue mixture.

8. Strain the excess liquid out of the cheesecloth and place the moist fabric over the skeleton's shoulders to cover it's back. Repeat with pieces of cheesecloth to cover the arms.

9. To create a reaper's hood, cut a piece of cheesecloth big enough for the hood, dip it in the glue, strain the excess, and place on top of the skull.

10. Cut strips of cheesecloth and hot glue them to the skeleton so they hang loose and give the decoration more life. Spray-paint the cheesecloth with gray or brown paint to give the fabric a weathered look (see page 67 for tips). You can also use an airbrush for better control.

11. Hang your skeleghost indoors to spook your guests when they enter your lair or outside so the wind can work dark magic with all of those hanging strands of cheesecloth.

Black Spider Prop

There is nothing like a giant spider to really creep out your guests, even the ones who aren't arachnophobes, and no better time than Halloween to add some goosebumps to the flesh of your unsuspecting friends. While this type of creepy crawly might fill most with fright, I personally find it a pure delight, so let this spider haunt a corner of your lair during Halloween and you just might lure like-minded, spider-loving boils and ghouls into your web.

You will need:

- One large balloon
- Paintbrush
- White school glue (e.g., Elmer's)
- Newspaper
- Paper towels
- 1-foot-long (0.3-meter-long) ¼-inch (6 mm) wooden dowel
- Expanding foam
- Hot glue gun and glue sticks
- One 3 x 5 x 2-inch (8 x 13 x 5 cm) piece of blue foam
- A rasp
- One 3 x 5 x 1-inch (8 x 13 x 2.5 cm) French oval wooden plaque
- A drill with a ¼-inch (6 mm) bit
- 16 feet (5 meters) of ¼-inch (6 mm) aluminum sculpture wire
- 16 feet (5 meters) of 1-inch (2.5 cm) foam pipe insulation
- Black electrical tape
- One 12 x 12 x 1-inch (30 x 30 x 2.5 cm) sheet of foam rubber
- Gloss black latex or acrylic paint
- One yard of synthetic black or gray fur
- Eight plastic hemispheres ranging from 1 to 3 inches (2.5 to 8 cm) in diameter
- Super glue

Directions:

1. Blow up the balloon so it's between 12 and 15 inches (30 and 38 cm) long. Use a paintbrush to apply a layer of white glue to the surface, then add strips of newspaper on top of the wet glue. Add more glue and more newspaper.
2. Once you have two layers of newspaper covering the entire balloon, you can switch to paper towels. Add a layer of glue and a layer of paper towels. Repeat with a second layer of the newspaper and then paper towels.
3. Allow the glue to dry. Once hardened, this orb will serve as the abdomen of your spider.
4. Insert the wooden dowel into the abdomen so that at least 3 inches (8 cm) are sticking out of it and fill the abdomen with expanding foam. Set aside until dry.

5. To create the cephalothorax, hot glue the blue foam to the wooden plaque and shape into a mound with a rasp.

6. Drill a ¼-inch (6 mm) hole in the side of the wooden plaque facing the abdomen and hot glue the wooden dowel into it, attaching the abdomen to the cephalothorax.

7. Cut 8 pieces of sculpture wire that are each 2 feet (0.6 meter) long. Drill ¼-inch (6 mm) holes in the wooden plaque where the legs will go in the sides of the cephalothorax and hot glue a wire into each hole.

8. Cut your foam pipe insulation into 8 lengths that are each 2 feet long (0.6 meter) and slip them onto the wire legs of your spider. Glue them into place with hot glue.

9. Wrap electrical tape very tightly around the foam at the ends of the legs to give them a tapered appearance. Using an image of a spider as reference, wrap electrical tape everywhere there should be a joint in the legs to make the legs look segmented.

10. Cut two pieces of sculpture wire that are 6 inches (15 cm) long each. Cut a long, thin strip from the sheet of foam rubber and wrap it around 4 inches (10 cm) of one of the wires, leaving 2 inches (5 cm) of wire exposed at the base. While holding the wrapped foam in place, tightly wrap black electrical tape around the foam to hold it in place. Repeat on the second piece of wire, and you'll now have two pedipalps.

11. Drill two ¼-inch (6 mm) holes in the front of the cephalothorax where you wish to place the pedipalps. Insert the pedipalps and glue in place with hot glue.

12. Paint your entire spider with gloss black latex or acrylic paint.

13. Cut strips of artificial fur that are 2 to 3 inches (5 to 8 cm) wide and about 7 inches (18 cm) long. Use hot glue to attach the strips of fur around the legs anywhere there is a joint. You can also add fur to the pedipalps if you wish.

14. For the eyes, paint the insides of the plastic hemispheres with gloss black paint. Glue them onto the face of your spider with super glue and your creepy crawly is finished!

Note: For a tarantula look, cover the tops of the cephalothorax and abdomen with fur, securing it in place with hot glue. For a black widow spider look, leave those parts bare and instead paint a red hourglass on the abdomen. Whether your spider is furry or not, hang it up in a high corner of your lair, and things are sure to get hairy!

Pumpkin King Posable Figure

Earlier in the book, I said I'd be using my stop-motion animation model-making skills to create some creepy DIY projects for this book. For this project, we can use techniques similar to the ones they used on *Disney Tim Burton's The Nightmare Before Christmas* to make a pumpkin-headed scarecrow figure that's totally posable! This makes for a great Halloween dinner centerpiece.

You will need:

- About 5 feet (1.5 meters) of ¼-inch (6 mm) aluminum sculpture wire
- Needle-nose pliers with a cutting edge
- One tube of plumber's epoxy
- Half yard of 1-inch-thick (2.5 cm) foam rubber sheet
- A spool of nylon thread
- Liquid latex
- Sponge or foam rubber
- Real or artificial branches, each about 4 inches (10 cm) long
- Hot glue gun and glue sticks
- Annealed wire or electrical tape
- Acrylic paint in rustic tones (brown, gray, and/or muted green)
- Paintbrush
- Spray adhesive
- Scraps of burlap
- Artificial moss or straw
- Miniature artificial pumpkin
- Black marker
- Wooden base
- Screws/washers
- Brush-on paint, in color of choice

Directions:

1. Cut five pieces of sculpture wire with the following specs: 6 inches (15 cm) for the neck; 20 inches (51 cm) for the arms; 6 inches (15 cm) for the spine; and two pieces that are 12 inches (30 cm) long each for the legs.
2. Cut off a piece of plumber's epoxy about a quarter of the length of the tube, knead until thoroughly mixed, and form into a ball. In about one minute, it will turn into a rock, so it's important to work fast!
3. Insert the neck wire into the top of the ball, insert the spine wire into the bottom of the ball and press the middle of the arms wire into the center of the ball.
4. Once cured, your wires will be forever joined inside of a small rock. That rock will serve as the chest of your scarecrow.
5. Find a spot on the spine from which you'd like to see the legs sprouting. Trim the spine wire if it's too long. Mix up another ball of plumber's epoxy and embed the spine wire and the leg wires within it.

6. Cut the foam sheet into strips about 1 inch (2.5 cm) wide. Wrap one of the strips around the waist, working your way up toward the chest and onto one of the arms. Secure with nylon thread.

7. Repeat until all the limbs are covered and you've built up the scarecrow's body.

8. Pour a bit of liquid latex into a small cup or lid. Dip a sponge or a piece of foam rubber into the liquid latex and pat it on some newspaper until the sponge is nearly dry, then pat the sponge onto the figure to apply just a bit or liquid latex to your model. Let dry.

9. Create hands by attaching the small branches to the forearms of your character with hot glue and reinforce by wrapping annealed wire or electrical tape around them.

10. Apply acrylic paint to the body of your character with a brush. Let dry.

11. Spray your figure all over with spray adhesive and let dry.

12. Cut strips of burlap to create clothing for the scarecrow. Spray the back of the burlap with spray adhesive and allow it to dry. Once dry, attach the burlap to the model.

13. Attach artificial moss or straw coming out from the clothing. Secure with hot glue.

14. Draw a creepy jack-o'-lantern face on your miniature pumpkin with a pencil, then go over the final design with a black marker.

15. Make a hole in the bottom of the pumpkin head and glue the pumpkin onto the neck wire.

16. To mount your figure to a wooden base, twist the ends of the leg wires into loops about the size of a penny. Bend them at 90-degree angles to serve as feet. Place them on your wooden base and screw into the wood, using metal washers to keep the screws above the feet wires.

17. Paint your wooden base with a brush-on paint in a color of your choosing.

Note: You can modify this project further by creating the scarecrow's wooden cross out of easy-to-carve balsa wood and by decorating the wooden base with dirt, skulls, graves or whatever will make it extra creepy! You can even use the techniques demonstrated in the Gothic Birdhouse project (page 86) to make that base a graveyard!

➤ Warm Mulled Cider ◄

Yield: 6-8 servings

This is one of the *Gothic Homemaking* recipes that is the most shared! Every year, many of our viewers make this cozy beverage to get into the Halloween mood. But this warm, fragrant drink is great to enjoy all through the fall and winter months. It's just as good during Creepy Christmas!

Ingredients:

- ½ gallon (2 L) unfiltered apple cider
- 15–20 whole cloves
- 1 whole orange
- 1 apple, sliced
- 6 whole cardamom seeds
- 13 dried allspice berries
- 4 cinnamon sticks, plus more for garnish
- ¼ tsp freshly ground nutmeg
- 2 star anise pods
- 1 Tbsp dark brown sugar

Directions:

1. Place a large pot on the stove at medium heat. Add the apple cider to the pot.
2. Stick the whole cloves into the orange.
3. Add the orange and apple slices to the pot.
4. Add the cardamom seeds, dried allspice berries, and cinnamon sticks and stir well.
5. Add the nutmeg, star anise, and sugar, stirring regularly.
6. Let the cider simmer for 45 minutes.
7. Ladle the mulled cider into mugs and garnish each with a cinnamon stick. Serve warm.

Optional: Add an ounce (30 ml) of spiced rum to your mug for an extra holiday kick!

Halloween Scream Cocktail

Yield: 1 drink

A nicely balanced, potent spell will surely hit the spot of your adult guests. If you're looking for a libation that really captures the color, smells, and tastes of the season, look no further! This pumpkin-colored, Halloween-themed cocktail will really get your adult guests in the right spirit.

Ingredients:

- 1 ounce (30 ml) Captain Morgan spiced rum
- 1 ounce (30 ml) Hiram Walker pumpkin liqueur
- 1 ounce (30 ml) Fireball Cinnamon Whisky
- 3 ounces (90 ml) apple cider
- Juice of ½ orange
- Juice of ½ lime
- ½ ounce (15 ml) Falernum
- A splash of allspice dram (optional)
- Ice
- Slice of orange, for garnish
- Fresh nutmeg, for garnish (optional)

Directions:

1. In a cocktail shaker, combine the spiced rum, pumpkin liqueur, whisky, apple cider, orange and lime juices, and Falernum, along with the allspice dram, if desired.
2. Add ice and shake. Double strain into a martini glass and garnish with the orange slice and fresh nutmeg, if desired.

Poltergeist Punch

Yield: 6-8 servings

Of course, not everyone at your affair will be an imbiber of spirits, so it's good to have a beverage on hand that looks and tastes just as wonderfully monstrous as a Halloween cocktail with none of the bite.

Ingredients:

- 1 ¾ pints (1 L) grape juice
- 3 ½ pints (2 L) ginger ale
- ½ gallon (2 L) Hawaiian Punch Green Berry Rush
- 2 cups (480 ml) pineapple juice
- 16 sour black licorice laces
- 10 green sour apple laces

Directions:

1. Fill a skull-shaped silicon mold with grape juice and freeze.
2. Pour the ginger ale into a large glass bowl. Add the Hawaiian Punch and pineapple juice, then set in refrigerator to chill.
3. When ready to serve, braid groups of four black licorice laces together and hang from the sides of the bowl to give the bowl the appearance of a tentacled terror.
4. Add the skull ice cube to the punch to give this murky mixture some menace!

Optional: Consider decorating the table with some fake creepy crawlies and dry ice for an added ghostly touch. (Remember: use caution when handling dry ice and do not ingest it.)

The Devil's Eggs

Yield: 12 deviled eggs

With just a dash of food coloring, you can make traditional deviled eggs even more devilish for your Halloween soiree! If you like yours hot and spicy, feel free to turn up the heat by adding chili powder or Tabasco. You can also experiment with different food colorings to create a dish that fits your color scheme.

Ingredients:

- 6 hard-boiled eggs, cooled
- Red and black food coloring
- 4 Tbsp mayonnaise
- 1 Tbsp white vinegar
- 1 Tbsp Dijon mustard
- Salt and pepper

Directions:

1. Lightly crack the shells of your cooled hard-boiled eggs all over with the back of a spoon. Place the eggs in a bowl of room temperature water dyed with about a tablespoon of red food coloring. Place the bowl in the refrigerator for 6 hours.
2. Once the dye has worked its magic, remove the bowl from the refrigerator and carefully peel the shells off the eggs. They should now have a wonderfully creepy design of red lines where the coloring seeped in through the cracks.
3. Halve the eggs and remove the yolks, setting them aside in a small bowl. To dye the tops of the egg whites red, place them face down on a dish containing 1 teaspoon of water and 1 teaspoon of red food coloring.
4. Mash the yolks and mix in the mayonnaise, vinegar, and mustard until smooth. Season with salt and pepper to taste.
5. Add about 8 drops of red food coloring and 8 drops of black food coloring to the mixture, then spoon or pipe about a tablespoon of the dark red filling into the scooped-out egg whites.

10

Creepy Christmas

alloween is barely over when you begin to hear Christmas music oozing from the speakers at your local stores. To many spooky lifestylers, these overly-sweet ditties are like wolfsbane to a werewolf. But at the Lair of Voltaire, we've been celebrating a spooky version of the festive holiday for a few years now, what we ghouls call Creepy Christmas!

Once upon a time, I was certainly one of those people who dreaded the extremely unspooky trappings of Christmas. The first spark of change came back in 2008, when I was invited to contribute a short film to the Creepy Christmas Film Festival created by New York City filmmakers Beck Underwood and Larry Fessenden. My entry was a spooky stop-motion film called *X-Mess Detritus*, narrated by My Chemical Romance frontman Gerard Way. Before then, I don't think I could find a way to get excited about Christmas.

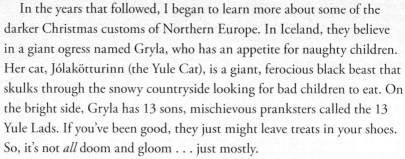

In the years that followed, I began to learn more about some of the darker Christmas customs of Northern Europe. In Iceland, they believe in a giant ogress named Gryla, who has an appetite for naughty children. Her cat, Jólakötturinn (the Yule Cat), is a giant, ferocious black beast that skulks through the snowy countryside looking for bad children to eat. On the bright side, Gryla has 13 sons, mischievous pranksters called the 13 Yule Lads. If you've been good, they just might leave treats in your shoes. So, it's not *all* doom and gloom . . . just mostly.

The Germans have Frau Perchta, sometimes described as a pagan goddess, sometimes as a witch or a half-demon/half woman monster. Whatever her appearance, she's always on the lookout for unruly and naughty children when night falls during the twelve days of Christmas. It is said that when she finds one, she will slit open the child's belly and tear out his innards. She then stuffs the child's belly with straw, rocks, and rubbish and sews it shut. Merry Christmas!

And most famous of all the European Christmas monsters to make their way to American shores is Krampus. How could Europe have kept this delightful beast from us for all these centuries? Like many of the monsters above, Krampus serves as a Christmastime boogeyman, threatening children who do not behave with terrifyingly severe punishments. While the jolly and benevolent Saint Nicholas comes on December 6th to bring presents to well-behaved children, the night before, on Krampusnacht (Krampus Night), his black, furry, demonic counterpart with goat horns and hooves arrives. It is believed that Krampus beats bad children with birch branches, chains them up, and tosses them into a sack or basket on his back to be eaten, drowned, or transported to Hell. *So be good, for goodness' sake!*

In recent years, this Yuletide monster has become increasingly popular in the United

States, bolstered by appearances in Christmas-themed horror films (see a list of them later in the chapter). It has now become fairly common in the States to find Krampus-themed dolls, ornaments, and decorations. Furthermore, while haunted attractions used to only operate during the Halloween season, this newfound enthusiasm for Krampus and horror-related Christmas themes has inspired a wave of Christmastime haunts around the country.

But if you can't find a spooky Christmas haunt near you, you can still join in on the fun!

Your Creepy Christmas Tree

A Creepy Christmas starts in the home, and just like the holiday that inspired it, the Christmas tree will be at the center of your decorations. Of course, by the time we're done, it might look more like a Cryptmas tree! As with all Gothic homemaking, the first thing we need to consider is the color scheme, so you can purchase a fitting tree.

Green tree: Is it impossible to turn this most common Christmas tree into a Gothic tree? No. But it is challenging. For this reason, I feel it's preferable to buy a tree in a color that is better suited for dark decorating. Of course, that also means foregoing a natural tree in favor of an artificial one.

Black tree: A black tree makes a very bold statement and will certainly convey to your guests that they've entered a home where Christmas is served with an extra helping of creepy. When decorating a black tree, I suggest white, silver, gold, or even red decorations for a classic Gothic look. Black decorations on a black tree, while they may be hard to spot, can also make for an intense look. If you prefer your decorations to be black, then a tree of a lighter color might be a better choice.

Voltaire Says

As artificial trees are not as kind on the environment as live ones, I suggest buying something you can use year after year. At the Lair of Voltaire, we have a white one that has served us well for creating a black and orange Halloween theme, a red and white Krampus theme, and a black and white classic Gothic tree.

Red, pink, and purple trees: A red Christmas tree covered in black ornaments will add the perfect touch to your vampiric lair. A purple tree with silver or gold and black ornaments creates a decoration fit for darkside royalty. But pink? Can that really work? Pastel Goths everywhere will say, "Absolutely!" Add black bats, little black coffins, and white skulls to a pink tree to create the perfect cross of cute and creepy. Perfect for Countess Barbie in her castle in Malibu, Transylvania.

White tree: A white tree might not seem like the obvious choice for a spooky look, but I feel it's the best! White presents a blank canvas upon which to place bold black ornaments and really make them the focus. When using a black tree, it's the tree itself that communicates the spookiness. On a white tree, you can really let the decorations tell their scary stories. Black spiders, coffins, bats, and the like really pop on this Creepy Christmas tree. That bold impact and the tree's versatility are why we chose a white tree for our home.

Dark the Halls

Once you have your tree, you'll need some eerie ornaments! Over the years, I've had luck sourcing some spooky ones from surprising places. Here are a few spots to try for dark decorations for your Cryptmas tree.

Etsy: A quick search for "Gothic ornaments" will produce a slew of results on this site! You can find everything from ornately sculpted spheres with a skull motif to some spooky stained-glass offerings, and there's no shortage of dangly skeletons and hanging bats to add to your spooky tree. Plus, since most of what's on Etsy is handmade by independent artists, you can feel good about supporting a small business and likely contributing to an artist being able to provide their families with holiday gifts of their own!

Gothic brands: Sometimes, large Gothic brands get in the horrorday spirit. In years past, Blackcraft Cult has offered some really nice ceramic ornaments featuring bats, Krampus, Edgar Allan Poe, Baphomet, and a cat named Lucipurr. Killstar has also released cranium glass ornaments, Dracul ornaments, and a series of spooky spheres bedecked in macabre motifs. And who knows, perhaps by the time this book comes out, there will be something elegantly creepy for your tree from the Lair of Voltaire!

Morawski Ornaments: Every Halloween, I head to the John Derian store in New York City to see their barren tree full of an incredible selection of high-end, hand-blown glass ornaments of bats, skeletons, and other ghoulish creatures. These incredible ornaments are handmade in Poland by Morawski Ornaments. And when Christmas creeps around, John Derian doesn't take them down . . . they put up *more*. I have purchased about a dozen different bat ornaments and a large handful of Krampus ones, which I featured in an episode of *Gothic Homemaking* called "Our Scary Christmas Tree." As our spooky subculture is so small, it's extremely rare to find things that are elegant and high quality as well as being macabre.

Boo It Yourself

As always, if you can't find it, make it! It's remarkably easy to make creepy Cryptmas ornaments and decor of your own—you just need to keep your peepers open around Halloween!

Treat yourself to some Gothic ornaments, no matter what kind of tree you deck!

Safety First

Read all safety notices on your materials and tools and ensure you have the proper protective gear before getting started. See page 66 for other helpful reminders and tips.

Scary Christmas Skull Ornament

Using this technique, you can create scary skull ornaments for your tree that will look both creepy and elegant, and no one will know you spent mere pennies and just a few minutes on each one! Purchase the skulls you'll need for this project from a big craft store at Halloween.

You will need:

- Twelve eye screws
- Twelve plastic skulls about 3 inches (7.6 cm) in diameter
- Superglue
- Black lacquer spray paint
- Silver wax metallic finish (e.g., Rub 'n Buff)
- Paintbrush
- About 72 inches (183 cm) of ⅛-inch (3 mm) thick ribbon in color of your choice
- Twelve silver ornament hooks

Directions:

1. Screw an eye screw into the top of each skull and glue in place with superglue. Spray-paint the skulls black (see page 67 for tips).
2. Once dry, dry-brush the silver wax metallic finish onto the skulls.
3. Cut a 6-inch (15 cm) piece of ribbon. Thread it through the eye screw and tie the ends together to create a loop. Attach an ornament hook to your ribbon and hang on the tree.

Glitter Bat Ornaments

In 2020, we made a tree that was Halloween-themed, with a black-and-orange color scheme on our white tree, and I came up with this deceptively simple and inexpensive way to make elegant, sparkly bat ornaments for our spooky tree.

You will need:

- Twelve 9 x 12-inch (23 x 30 cm) peel and stick black glitter foam sheets (I suggest the ones from Creatology)
- 9 x 12-inch (23 x 30 cm) sheet of construction paper for making a template
- Metallic permanent marker
- Scissors
- Twelve 2mm red (or any color) crystals
- Beacon Magna-Tac 809 (or any glue recommended for crystals and foam)
- Twelve silver ornament hooks

Directions:

1. Peel the adhesive off two pieces of the glitter foam and stick together.
2. On a piece of construction paper, draw a bat shape that's roughly 9 inches (23 cm) long. Once you have an image of a bat shape in the desired size, cut out with scissors to use as a template.
3. Place your bat template on the double-sided glitter foam and trace with a metallic marker, then cut out your sparkly bat with scissors.
4. Glue two crystals to your glittery bat with Beacon Magna-Tac 809 for the eyes.
5. Poke a hole in the foam just above the eyes with any sharp tool or even the ornament hook itself, thread an ornament hook through the hole, and hang on the tree.

Kreepy Krampus Coaster Ornaments

As I mentioned above, in 2022, our creepy Christmas tree had a dozen or so Krampus ornaments from Poland. These gorgeous, hand-blown glass pieces are as expensive as they are precious. But you don't need to break the bank to add everyone's favorite Christmas boogeyman to your Cryptmas tree. To begin, you'll need some really great, especially old-timey, illustrations of Krampus. You can purchase Krampus postcards or print out high-resolution images from the good old internet.

You will need:

- Six or more 4-inch (10 cm) square cardboard paper coasters
- Six or more Krampus illustrations, roughly 4 inches (10 cm) square
- Spray adhesive or a glue stick
- Acrylic paint (any color)
- 2-inch (5 cm) chip brush
- A hole puncher or ⅛-inch (3 mm) drill bit and drill
- 36 inches (91 cm) of ⅛-inch (3 mm) ribbon
- Six or more ornament hooks

Directions:

1. Place a coaster on one of your illustrations and trace the edges. Use this as a guide to trim the illustration so it's the same size as the coaster.
2. Use spray adhesive or a glue stick to attach the illustration to the coaster, illustrated side out, then paint the back of the coaster. Let dry.
3. Use the hole puncher or drill bit to make a hole near the top center of the coaster.
4. Cut a 6-inch (15 cm) piece of ribbon and thread it through the hole, then tie the ends to form a loop. Attach an ornament hook and your Krampus ornament is ready to hang.

Optional: Make your Kreepy Krampus Coaster Ornaments more elegant by adding an ornate lace or ribbon frame around the picture. You can also make each ornament double-sided by simply adding an image to both sides of the coaster!

Spooky Santa Skeletons Ornament

Another item I pick up every Halloween are little plastic skeletons. I find they are incredibly useful for all kinds of DIY projects, including this one! This is a similar technique to the Scary Christmas Skull ornaments (page 160), but feature the full skeleton body—and festive yet creepy Santa hats. You'll be making two variations of these skeletons for your tree, because variety is the spice of life!

You will need:

- Twelve eye screws
- Twelve plastic skeletons about 4 inches (10 cm) tall
- Superglue
- Black lacquer spray paint
- Silver wax metallic finish (e.g., Rub 'n Buff)
- Black acrylic paint
- Paintbrush
- One sheet of 9 x 12-inch (23 x 30 cm) black felt
- Twelve silver ornament hooks
- Needle-nose pliers
- Hot glue gun and glue sticks
- 6 white and 6 black mini poms-poms (I recommend the ones from Creatology)
- One sheet of 9 x 12-inch (23 x 30 cm) white felt

Directions:

1. Screw the eye screws into the top of the heads of all 12 skeletons and glue in place with superglue. Spray-paint 6 of the skeletons black (see page 67 for tips).
2. Once the black skeletons are dry, dry-brush silver wax metallic finish onto each and then set aside to dry.
3. For the other 6 skeletons, you can use them as is or brush black acrylic paint onto them, then wipe off most of the paint with a sponge or paper towel to add depth and dimension. Set aside to dry.
4. For the Santa hats for the white skeletons, cut 12 triangles from the black felt that are each about 1 inch (2.5 cm) wide and 2.5 inches (6 cm) tall. All 12 triangles should be identical, so feel free to use a template.
5. Attach an ornament hook to the eye screw of one of the white skeletons and tighten the ornament hook in place with needle-nose pliers. Hot-glue one of the black felt triangles to the back of the skeleton's head to make the back of the Santa hat.
6. Glue a second black felt triangle to the front of the skeleton's head to be the front of the hat, sandwiching the ornament hook between the two felt pieces.

7. Thread a white mini pom-pom down from the top of the ornament hook until it rests on top of the black felt Santa hat and glue in place.

8. Cut a piece of white felt, 3 inches (8 cm) long and ¼ inch (6 mm) tall, and glue onto the black felt, around the skull, to become the white rim of the hat.

9. Repeat steps 4 to 7 for all six white skeletons.

10. To make hats for the black skeletons, repeat steps 4 to 7, but make the triangles out of white felt, use a black mini pom-pom for the top of the hat, and make the trim out of black felt.

Tip: For a more classic look, you can make all the Santa hats out of red felt with white felt trim and white mini pom-poms. Either way, a dozen or so Spooky Santa Skeletons are coming to town!

Sinister Snowman Prop

Until the big day arrives, there will be curious eyes peering at those waiting presents day and night, wondering what wonders they hold. I find it's prudent to have a Sinister Snowman stand guard and make sure no one tries to shake, rattle, and roll the boxes to guess at what's inside. This frightfully frozen fellow is remarkably easy to make and starts with some items sourced around Halloween, with three big, white artificial pumpkins making up the body of our abominable friend.

So . . . do you want to build a snowman?

You will need:

- 3-inch (7 cm) hole saw
- One large white artificial pumpkin
- One medium white artificial pumpkin
- One small white artificial pumpkin
- Pencil
- Dremel tool with a cutting blade attachment
- Drill with drill bits and paddle bits of various sizes
- Twelve plastic icicle decorations
- Two black artificial branches
- Black matte or satin finish spray paint
- Two tubes of plumber's epoxy
- Black acrylic paint
- 2-inch (5 cm) chip brush
- A tube of E6000 craft glue
- A small fascinator top hat to fit atop your snowman
- Small broom prop

Directions:

1. Use the hole saw to make holes in the bottom of all three pumpkins.
2. Draw a jack-o'-lantern face on the smallest pumpkin in pencil. Cut out the mouth and eyes using a Dremel tool. Use a paddle bit on a drill to make a hole for the nose, the size of one of the icicle decorations.
3. Trim the artificial branches to a fitting snowman-arm length, then spray-paint them black (see page 67 for tips).
4. While they dry, drill holes that are slightly smaller than the diameter of your artificial branches in the sides of the middle pumpkin. Stick the branches into the holes.
5. Break off 2-inch (5 cm) pieces of the plumber's epoxy. Knead thoroughly and before it becomes hard, shape into a lump of coal and press onto the front of your medium pumpkin. Add two "coal" buttons each to the medium and large pumpkins, then paint them black with acrylic paint.
6. Glue the medium pumpkin on top of the large one and the small onto the medium with E6000 craft glue.

7. Insert an icicle into the nose hole on the smallest pumpkin and glue in place, if necessary. Cut down 8 plastic icicles to create teeth for your snowman and glue them into the mouth.

8. Remove the headband from the miniature top-hat fascinator and glue the hat onto the snowman's head.

9. Place the small broom in the branchy fingers of your snowman and display.

Tip: For an extra fancy snowman, cut a length of 3-inch wired ribbon about a yard long and wrap it around the snowman's neck, then shape to mimic a scarf blowing in the icy wind.

Other Tree Decorating Tips

These simple ornament tutorials will help you get your spooky tree into shape, but ornaments are only part of it! Here are some other ideas to fill out your frightful fir.

Beauty garland: Wrap a garland of fall leaves around your Christmas tree for a wonderfully warm look. You also don't have to stop at fall colors. In 2022, I used a garland of poinsettias (with all the green parts painted black) for our red and black Krampus-themed tree.

Let there be (spooky) lights: String lights are important Christmas tree decorations for most people, but little multicolored blinking lights hardly convey a Gothic feel. Instead, during the Halloween season, I stock up on jack-o'-lantern-, skeleton-, and bat-shaped string lights to illuminate my Creepy Christmas!

Chasing skirts: The classic tree skirt hides the tree base. For a Gothic look, source one that's black. You can also simply select a fantastic Gothic fabric (or even a tablecloth!) that matches your color scheme and use that as the tree skirt. No cutting or sewing required—just bunch it up under the tree like a spooky scarf.

This is a Thing Called a Present . . .

Once your tree is ready, you'll want your wrapped presents to match. Find monochromatic paper in black, white, and gray, and you will be on your way to wrapping classic Gothic presents. Match black paper with a white bow, then white paper with a black bow. Wrap other presents in solid gray paper and alternate using black, white, and gray bows. Mixing and matching the paper and bows in these three tones will give you a wonderfully spooky pile of presents suitable for Frankenstein to give the Wolfman. (And yes, of course you can use black paper with a black blow for that über-Goth look!) For a more elegant touch, add silver or gold into the mix.

Creepy Christmas Cinema

There's no better way to spend a cold winter's night than snuggling up on the couch in a cozy, creepy comforter with a fellow horror fan or two for movie night. When it comes to spooky Christmas movies, nothing beats *Disney Tim Burton's The Nightmare Before Christmas* for me! There is no better example of a film that so fully imbues Christmas with our love for Halloween, and despite being about creatures that live to scare mortals, this story is overwhelmingly wholesome and fun for the whole family. Of course, as a stop-motion animator myself, I have a soft spot for this film!

Another stop-motion classic to share with little monsters is the 1964 Rankin and Bass classic *Rudolph the Red-Nosed Reindeer.* The Abominable Snow Monster in the film will serve as a gateway to future creature-feature viewing. The Island of Misfit Toys also hit a young outcast like me hard, and to this day reminds me of the spooky community we've built. I also recommend digging up Rankin and Bass's *Mad Monster Party*, one of the films that inspired *The Nightmare Before Christmas.*

A skirt really pulls any outfit together.

Once the little monsters are tucked into their beds with visions of gremlins and Abominable Snow Monsters rampaging in their heads, you can enjoy your favorite Christmasy horror films. Try these holiday screamers:

- *Better Watch Out* (2016)
- *Anna and the Apocalypse* (2017)
- *Christmas Bloody Christmas* (2022)
- *Black Christmas* (1974)
- *All the Creatures Were Stirring* (2018)
- *Silent Night* (2012)
- *Holiday Hell* (2019)

Holiday decorating and movie nights are always more fun with some seasonal treats! I have a few tips for putting a terrifying twist on some holiday favorites that Yule love.

Santa Skull Cookies

Yield: 12 cookies

During this time of year, you should be able to find a cookie cutter in the shape of Santa's head, complete with his iconic hat. You can use one of these and your favorite sugar cookie recipe (or mine below) to morph old Saint Nick into a macabre skull in a festive cap!

Ingredients:

SUGAR COOKIE DOUGH

- 1 egg
- 1 ½ cups (181 g) powdered sugar
- 1 cup (227 g) softened butter
- ½ tsp almond extract
- 1 tsp vanilla extract
- 2 ½ cups (313 g) all-purpose flour, plus extra for dusting

- 1 tsp cream of tartar
- 1 tsp baking soda

ICING
- 3–5 Tbsp milk
- 3 cups (363 g) powdered sugar
- ¼ tsp vanilla extract
- Black food coloring

Directions:

1. To make the cookies: Add the egg, powdered sugar, butter, almond extract, and vanilla extract to a large bowl and mix with an electric mixer. Once thoroughly mixed, slowly stir in the flour, cream of tartar, and baking soda.

2. Separate the dough into two halves. Flatten each piece into a disc, then wrap the dough in plastic wrap and put in the refrigerator for at least 2 hours.

3. When you're ready to continue, heat your oven to 375°F (190°C, gas mark 5).

4. Roll out the dough on a lightly floured surface until it's about a ¼ inch (6 mm) thick, then cut out as many Santa cookies as you can. Place them on ungreased cookie sheets, at least 2 inches (5 cm) apart.

5. Bake the cookies for 6–8 minutes or until the edges are golden brown. Place aside to cool.

6. To make the icing: Add the milk, powdered sugar, and vanilla into a small bowl and mix with a spoon until smooth.

7. Pour half the icing into another small bowl. Add 6 drops of black food coloring into the second bowl and stir until thoroughly mixed. Add more if necessary to create a rich, dark black.

8. With either a spoon or a piping bag, add the white icing to the face of the cookie and black icing to the hat part of the cookie. With a piping bag, add details to the skull (like the eyes, nose, and teeth) with the black icing.

9. Let the cookies stand about 4 hours or until the icing is thoroughly dry before serving.

Ginger-dead Men

Yield: 12 cookies

Run, run, run, as fast as you can, you can't catch me, I'm the Ginger-*dead* Man! Gingerbread cookies are fun, but not nearly creepy enough for ghouls like us. Use this recipe to create an army of undead skeletons that are ready to march their spicy deliciousness right into your mouth.

Ingredients:

Cookies

- 3 cups (376 g) all-purpose flour, plus extra for dusting
- 1 tsp baking soda
- ¼ tsp salt
- 2 tsp ground ginger
- 1 tsp ground cinnamon
- ¼ tsp ground nutmeg
- ¾ cup (170 g) softened butter
- ¾ cup (146 g) brown sugar
- 1 egg
- ½ cup (156 g) molasses
- 1 tsp vanilla extract

Icing

- 3–5 Tbsp milk
- 3 cups (363 g) powdered sugar
- ¼ tsp vanilla extract
- Black food coloring

Directions:

1. To make the cookies: In a large bowl, mix the flour, baking soda, salt, ginger, cinnamon, and nutmeg.
2. In another bowl, use an electric mixer to beat the butter and brown sugar until fluffy. Add the egg, molasses, and vanilla and continue to mix. Gradually work in the flour mixture on low speed until fully integrated.
3. Flatten the dough into a flat disc and wrap it in plastic wrap. Refrigerate for a minimum of 4 hours.
4. When ready to proceed, heat your oven to 350°F (180°C, gas mark 4).
5. Roll out the dough on a lightly floured surface until the dough is about ¼ inch (6 mm) thick. Use a gingerbread man cookie cutter to cut out your little men, then place them about 2 inches (5 cm) apart on an ungreased baking sheet.
6. Bake for 8–10 minutes or until the edges are golden brown, then place on wire racks to cool.
7. To make the icing: Add the milk, powdered sugar, and vanilla into a small bowl and mix with a spoon until smooth.

8. Pour half the icing into another small bowl. Add 6 drops of black food coloring into the second bowl and stir until thoroughly mixed. Add more if necessary to create a rich, dark black.

9. With either a spoon or a piping bag, add a layer of the black icing to coat each cookie front. Put the white icing into a piping bag and useto create a skull, bones, and ribs on each Ginger-dead Man.

10. Let the cookies stand about 4 hours or until the icing is thoroughly dry before serving.

Tip: You can also make ginger-bats, if those strike your fancy. Just grab a bat-shaped cookie cutter!

Netherworld Nog

Yield: 8 servings

What do you wash down Ginger-dead Men with? Why, Netherworld Nog of course!
Personally, I've always been a fan of eggnog. That thick, comforting drink smells
and tastes like Christmas and really embodies the mood of the season. But if we're
celebrating a Creepy Christmas, we simply *have* to make our eggnog quite a bit more
eerie—and I know just how to do that!

Ingredients:

- 4 cups (950 ml) milk
- 2 ½ tsp vanilla extract, divided
- 1 tsp ground cinnamon
- 7 whole cloves
- 12 large egg yolks
- 1 ½ cups (301 g) white sugar
- 4 cups (950 ml) light cream
- ¾ tsp ground nutmeg
- Black food coloring
- Canned whipped cream
- 1 Tbsp black edible glitter
- 1 Tbsp black pearl sugar sprinkles

Directions:

1. Heat the milk, ½ teaspoon vanilla extract, cinnamon, and cloves in a saucepan
   for 5 minutes on the lowest heat, stirring constantly. Slowly increase the heat and
   bring to a boil.

2. In a large bowl, whisk the egg yolks. Add the sugar and continue to whisk until
   light and fluffy.

3. Pour a bit of the hot milk mixture into the egg mixture while whisking quickly.
   Continue whisking while adding hot milk until you've added all the milk mixture
   to the eggs.

4. Pour the whole mixture into the saucepan. On medium heat, stir constantly for
   about 3 minutes or until the mixture becomes thick. Do not allow the liquid to boil.

5. Strain the liquid to remove the cloves and set aside to cool for at least 1 hour.

6. Once cool, stir in the cream, then add the nutmeg and remaining 2 teaspoons
   of vanilla.

7. To give your nog a ghoulish appearance, add 4 or more drops of black food
   coloring and stir. Refrigerate your gray nog for at least two hours.

8. When you are ready to serve your drinks, pour the gray eggnog into a mug and
   top with whipped cream. Sprinkle a pinch of black glitter on the surface and
   decorate with black pearl sugar sprinkles.

Optional: If you like your eggnog spiked, add 2 cups (480 ml) of rum to the mixture. Alternatively, you can just add one or two ounces (30–60 ml) of rum to each glass for those who wish to imbibe.

Part 4
Inspiration and Exploration

11

Spooky Pastimes and Travel

The world is full of fascinating, phantasmagorical places steeped in spookiness. I've visited a few cities in America that embrace their dark history rather than shy away from it, explored the unique burial rituals of Indonesian tribes, and, as I now live in Mexico several months of the year, have explored their intimate relationship with the concept of death. Beyond filling my life with countless hours of entertainment and joy, traveling to these places has been inspiring and eye-opening. I've compiled here a short list of some of my favorite stops, so let's spread our bat wings and fly!

America

Sleepy Hollow, New York

You've probably heard of "The Legend of Sleepy Hollow" by Washington Irving, which gave the world the infamous Headless Horseman. The titular town has become a major Halloween destination, visited by horror fans and spooky influencers alike. At Halloween, there are haunted hayrides, a jack-o'-lantern blaze, and a parade. At Sleepy Hollow Cemetery, you'll find the Old Dutch burial grounds and guides who can take you to the graves of the real people who possibly inspired the characters from Irving's story. It's even believed that the headless Hessian soldier rumored to be the Headless Horseman is buried there in an unmarked grave. Don't forget to pay your respects at the grave of the legendary author who put this town on the map, or tour Washington Irving's estate.

I love when a town embraces their spooky heritage, and this town chose to do exactly that in 1996. That's the year the town's name was officially changed to Sleepy Hollow, the name Irving gave it in his short story. Previously, it was simply North Tarrytown.

PREVIOUS: Monsters on parade for Balinese new year.

ABOVE: A grave in the Old Dutch burial grounds of Sleepy Hollow Cemetery.

Salem, Massachusetts

During the Salem witch trials of 1692, over two hundred people were accused of being in league with the devil. Nineteen souls were hanged by the neck until dead and several more died while being tortured or in jail. Today, Salem has adopted the image of the witch on everything from sports teams to police cars. There's a bronze statue of *Bewitched* actress Elizabeth Montgomery as her witchy character Samantha Stephens atop a broom right in the center of town, surrounded by witchcraft, holistic healing, Gothic, and vampiric stores. Ironically, Salem is now a place where the witch is seen as a benevolent healer, practicing an art that is celebrated instead of persecuted. Take *that*, 1692!

Naturally, Salem has become a Halloween hot spot. Store after store is filled with candles and essential oils, spells and pentagrams, spooky frocks, and frightful figurines. As for sightseeing, try the Salem Witch

The iconic *Bewitched* statue in Salem.

Museum, the House of the Seven Gables (immortalized in the Nathanial Hawthorne book of the same), and the Witch House, the home of one of the judges from the 1692 witch trials. Visit *Hocus Pocus* filming locations like Pioneer Village and the Dennison House, or find a ghost or other supernatural-themed tour that piques your interest.

The entrance to St. Rochs Cemetery in the Bywater district of New Orleans.

New Orleans, Louisiana

Nestled on the Mississippi River near the Gulf of Mexico, New Orleans was founded in 1718 by the French but passed through Spanish hands before eventually becoming part of the United States during the Louisiana Purchase. The mixture of Cajun, Spanish, African, Asian, and Native American cultures makes New Orleans unique. Known for its decadent creole cuisine and its intoxicating jazz music, New Orleans might very well be the best place to go full-on hedonist before giving it all up for Lent. And millions do exactly that during Mardi Gras.

Vampires are so popular in New Orleans that there are vampire-themed parties, shops, and cafes. I suggest Boutique Du Vampyre on St. Ann Street. All the spooky alternative folks tend to hang out around lower Decatur, so head down there and stop into the Abbey or Aunt Tiki's, or venture just outside the quarter to the Goat on St. Bernard Street. You might even find me there—it's where I perform when I'm in town. And make sure to visit a cemetery! There are a few small cemeteries near the French Quarter, but for a grand experience, take a trip to Metairie Cemetery, which has the most grandiose marble tombs and statues in all New Orleans.

Los Angeles, California

Sunny Los Angeles hardly seems like the place for a ghoulish getaway, but it has plenty to offer! Visit Hollywood Forever Cemetery and pay your respects to horror great Peter Lorre and the very first horror hostess ever, Maila Nurmi, the inimitable Vampira. Check the cemetery's event calendar for music performances and film screenings you can enjoy while there. Next, do some spooky shopping for ghastly garments at Monster-A-

A crypt at Hollywood Forever Cemetery in Los Angeles.

GoGo, then get ready to fill your cabinet of curiosities with all manner of oddities at Memento Mori in Hollywood or Vulture Culture Oddities in Burbank. While you're in Burbank, peruse the Gothic goodies at Bearded Lady Vintage and Oddities, then head next door to their Mystic Museum for a horribly good time. When night falls, head over to Hollywood Boulevard for a bite at Beetle House, the Tim Burton-themed restaurant. And if it's a Saturday night, walk over to Boardner's by La Belle and dance the night away at Bar Sinister, the biggest local Goth party.

Mexico

Mexico City

In 2019 I arrived at customs at the Mexico City airport to find a folk-art-inspired mural that included a Día de los Muertos *ofrenda*, or altar for placing offerings. The altar depicted in the painting had exactly one skull on it. Scrawled across the forehead of this painted skull was the name *Aurelio*. It was right then that I knew I was home.

The dark music scene in Mexico City is much, much bigger than in the States, and it's not isolated to the youth. These black-clad denizens of the Goth scene are called Darks (because they like things that are dark). To say you're Gothic in Mexico City, you proclaim, "Yo soy Darks!" And while it may not be grammatically correct, it gets the point across.

Every Saturday there is a dark flea market called El Chopo in the Buena Vista neighborhood of Mexico City. While you're there, catch a spooky band or four on their live music stage. The rest of the week, you can check out Horror Boutique near Zocalo or the Doctor Frankenstein Shop in Roma for your dark duds. If you're hungry and in the Roma neighborhood, check out Cafe Bizarro. On weekends, head upstairs to their live venue, Foro Bizarro, to check out a dark band or to dance the night away to spooky '80s music. You can also head over to El Real Under in the Coyoacan neighborhood, the longest-running Goth night in Mexico City.

The mural that welcomed me to Mexico in 2019.

If you have a mind for beheadings, check out the torture museum in El Centro Historico or, for a headier experience, walk over to El Templo Mayor, an ancient pyramid excavated in the town square where you can see a stone version of the *tzompantli*, a tower of human skulls collected from prisoners of war or other sacrificed humans. If your thirst for knowledge about ritual death is insatiable, head over to the Museum of Anthropology to see statues of the frightful Aztec god of death, Mictlantecuhtli, as well as sacrificial daggers, places to hold the heart of the victim, and much more.

A celebratory Día de los Muertos decoration.

Día de los Muertos

Coinciding with the Christian Allhallowtide, Día de los Muertos (Day of the Dead) takes place on or around November 1st and 2nd. Many families in Mexico will set up an *ofrenda*, or altar, including photos of their dearly departed, candles, decorations such as *calaveras* (decorative skulls), *cempazuchitl* (marigolds), and food and drinks that their dearly departed enjoyed when alive, as an offering to those who've passed away. Entire families will visit their dead relatives in the cemetery, sometimes even staying at their graves for an overnight picnic. This festival is not usually solemn or (pardon the pun) dead serious. It's a joyous time, when families welcome back their deceased loved ones (and are very happy to do so). Mexico City is a fabulous place to experience Day of the Dead, but for a truly immersive experience, explore places like San Luis Potosí, Oaxaca, or Guanajuato.

The Mummies of Guanajuato

As the story goes, back in the 1800s, the government of Guanajuato, a town now about a four-hour car ride from Mexico City, implemented a tax on permanent burials. Basically, as long as a body was taking up space in the local cemetery, their loved ones were to pay a small tax to keep them there, sort of like paying rent on the plot. This may have been motivated by the cholera pandemic of 1829 to 1851. The sharp rise in human deaths led to a rise in demand for graveyard space. If a family was unable to pay, the remains of their loved one were removed so that another body could take their place.

One of the mummies of Guanajuato.

The climate in Guanajuato was such that bodies placed into tombs were perfectly preserved. Imagine the shock of the gravediggers when they removed the first body and found that it was mummified! Evicted mummies were placed inside a nearby building and, because they were rigid, propped up against a wall in a standing position. Eventually, there were so many of them that the gravediggers began charging a small fee to the morbidly curious to sneak a peek. In 1969, Museo de las Momias (Museum of the Mummies) was established. To this day, you can pay a small fee to peruse their collection of over one hundred human mummies.

Indonesia

Bali

A Hindu temple on Bratan Lake in Bali.

If you're not afraid to spend many hours on a plane, you can visit Bali, known as the Island of the Gods—a place with no shortage of demons! While most of Indonesia's 18,000 islands are Muslim, Bali has the distinction of being Hindu, though it's a version of the religion that incorporates many of the island's pre-Hindu animist beliefs. Millions of tourists visit Bali every year to enjoy pristine beaches, serene rice terraces, and luxurious tropical resorts. But religion is so important to the people of Bali that there are shrines and statues of deities (both good and evil) absolutely everywhere.

Rangda, the demon queen and embodiment of evil, is depicted as an old nude crone with pendulous breasts, long fingernails, and a horrible mouth full of fangs and tusks. She has an appetite for small children and lords over an army of evil witches called Leyaks. Take in a traditional folkloric dance at the Ubud Palace and you're likely to see Rangda do battle against the forces of good. Walk along the streets of Ubud and you'll see masks of Rangda in souvenir shops and folk-art stores.

Visiting Bali has taught me a whole new way to look at monsters and the macabre. I tell monster lovers like me to go to Bali for a holiday on the beach but stay for all the horrible beasts!

Giant Monsters on Parade!

Monster fans who happen to visit during Balinese new year (roughly mid-March) are in for an *enormous* treat. For months leading up to the holiday, each village in Bali builds one or more *ogoh ogoh*, monstrous effigies of demons that can range from a few meters high to several stories. Once the sun sets on New Year's Eve, the towering monsters are placed onto grids made of bamboo then hoisted onto the shoulders of two dozen or more men of the village. Illuminated by torchlight and flares, they are marched through the darkness of the village as an orchestra of youths plays a wonderfully cacophonous symphony full of banging drums and cymbals. At the first intersection, the men aggressively turn counter-clockwise three times. This is repeated at every intersection in the town, and the men dip and weave to disorient the demon so it can't find its way back to the village. Once at the edge of town, the *ogoh ogoh* are purposely crashed into the ground, beaten with sticks, and set on fire, cleansing the village of negative energies, preparing for a clean start in the new year.

▲ The *ogoh ogoh* parade on the eve of Nyepi in March 2023.

The Unburied of Terunyan

On the banks of a lake called Danau Batur is an ancient village called Terunyan. The people of this village, who call themselves the Bali Aga or the original people of Bali, say theirs is the oldest village on the island. That is perhaps why so many of their customs predate the arrival of Hinduism, especially their unique custom for burying the dead. There is an ancient banyan tree that grows in a cemetery on the island that the Bali Aga call Taru Menyan, which literally translates as "nice-smelling tree." It is believed that the tree magically gives off a beautiful aroma that is so pleasant, it masks the smell of human decomposition. When a member of the village dies, their body is placed on the open ground near this tree, covered only by a cloth and small canopy made of bamboo, and left to decompose naturally.

Skulls on the stone wall near Taru Menyan in Terunyan.

I once hired a guide to take me to Terunyan to see this for myself. When we arrived at the cemetery, I was shown the tree and saw roughly 11 human corpses on the ground before it. The most recent body was of someone who had died two months earlier, but I admit that I perceived no unpleasant smells, just the magical fragrance of the Taru Menyan. When needed, the oldest corpse is removed to make way for more, as the Bali Aga believe that it is the soul and not the corporeal body that is important. Bare bones are tossed into a

pile with other bones and the skull joins a pile of other skulls on a small stone wall nearby. Standing before a pile of actual human skulls gave me a whole new appreciation and broader understanding of death.

The infamous notice at the entryway to the Parisian Catacombs.

Europe

The Catacombs of Paris, France

One of the most Gothic stops in Europe is probably the Catacombs. Under the streets of Paris you will find endless tunnels full of human skulls. As you descend into this netherworld, you may see a sign that reads *Arrête! C'estêici l'empire de la Mort*—"Stop! This is the empire of the dead!" You will quickly see why! During the 1700s, due to overcrowding in Parisian cemeteries, bodies were dug up and their remains were deposited here. It is believed that the skulls of over six million humans decorate these subterranean crypts.

The Sedlec Ossuary in Sedlec, Czech Republic

As the story goes, in the thirteenth century, an abbot from Sedlec made a pilgrimage to the Holy Land and returned with a handful of soil from Golgotha, the site where Jesus Christ is believed to have been crucified.

All Saints Chapel in Sedlec Ossuary.

Upon returning to Sedlec, he sprinkled that dirt in the abbey cemetery. When word got out, absolutely everyone was dying to be buried there, which caused a huge influx of human remains into the small chapel. The Black Death only added to the enormous wave of skulls and bones coming their way. Ultimately, a woodcarver was asked to do something about the messy piles of remains and his solution was to organize them into chandeliers and other decorative elements.

A Massive Gothic Festival in Leipzig, Germany

When in Europe, hop over to Leipzig for Wave-Gotik-Treffen, the largest Gothic festival in the world! Held every year around May or June, this festival brings tens of thousands of black-clad Goths together for three days of morbid music, spooky shopping, and all around macabre merry-making. Not limited to strictly Gothic music or Gothrock, the festival features hundreds of bands playing at multiple venues in myriad dark music genres, plus a variety of Renaissance and Viking markets. Some of Leipzig's museums even get in on the fun, offering free admission to the festival attendees.

If you are involved in the Gothic subculture or want to be, an event like this is the perfect place to expand your knowledge and understanding of what it can mean to be Goth. You can learn about the music as you jump from venue to venue and scope out wardrobe inspirations from the tens of thousands of Goths from all over the world converging at this one festival. After feeling like the only creepy weirdo in your hometown, it's just great to finally be in a city where the barista at Starbucks is the *only* person not dressed like a vampire!

A steampunk picnic during Wave-Gotik-Treffen 2014.

Stoked for Bram Stoker in Whitby, England

In 1890, Bram Stoker was vacationing in the quaint seaside town of Whitby, and it seems likely that he heard of the Russian vessel the *Dmitry*, which ran aground carrying boxes of silver sand. Perhaps that ship was the inspiration for his fictional *Demeter*, which enters Whitby's port carrying coffins full of earth and one very hungry Count Dracula. It's believed that Stoker also found the name Dracula while doing research about the Romanian Prince of Walachia in the town's public library. Atop one of Whitby's famous cliffs is the skeleton of an abandoned abbey, said to be the inspiration for Carfax Abbey, the home Dracula purchases just north of London to be closer to his intended victims. You can climb the 199 steps to the top of the cliff to take in views of the destroyed abbey and its ancient burial grounds. The best time to visit Whitby is during one of their Gothic festivals held biannually. There's nothing more charming than seeing a gaggle of Goths in their dark, Victorian finery winding up and down the cobblestone streets with canes and parasols in hand.

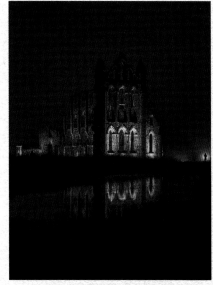

A spooky illuminated Whitby Abbey.

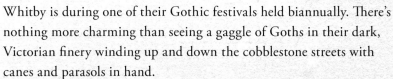

The 4:30 Movie

Growing up in the '70s and '80s, I lived for *The 4:30 Movie*, which had themed blocks of films throughout the week. I grew fond of the idea of curating a week's worth of horror films in the same genre. Consider doing the same at your lair! Pick five horror films in the same theme to screen each night of the week or create blocks of three for the weekend.

One of my favorites blocks is Tropical Horror, including:

- *I Walked with a Zombie* (1943)
- *White Zombie* (1932)
- *The Island of Lost Souls* (1932)
- *King Kong* (1933)
- *Voodoo Man* (1944)

Spooky Staycation

If travel is not your thing or is presently beyond your reach, fear not! There are many frightfully fun activities you can do without ever leaving your lair.

For starters, you can never go wrong with a good book. Brew up a nice mug of my warm mulled cider (page 150), wrap yourself in your favorite fleece, and choose a book depending on what kind of journey you'd like to go on. Try classics like *Dracula* by Bram Stoker, *Frankenstein* by Mary Shelley, or *The Strange Case of Dr. Jekyll and Mr. Hyde* by Robert Louis Stevenson. For a lesser-known vampire gem, try *Carmilla* by Sheridan Le Fanu. If you like things short and not-so-sweet, there are the short stories and poems of Edgar Allan Poe. For an out of this world but equally classic experience, try anything by H.P. Lovecraft. *The Call of Cthulhu* is my favorite and it's a fairly quick read. For modern horror, check out books by Anne Rice, Stephen King, and Clive Barker. And if you happen to enjoy campy but scary '80s horror stories about mall goths, zombies, and cryptids, check out my book *Call of the Jersey Devil*.

If you prefer to watch your horror, there are dozens of places to find a frightful film to stream, from mainstream platforms to horror-specific sites like Shudder and Screambox. If you really want to make it a special event, get a projector and a big white sheet and host a dastardly drive-in-themed party. If it's summer, hang the screen in the backyard and show a summer slasher, or during the Halloween season, host an indoor screening of a seasonal favorite like *Trick 'r Treat*, *Hocus Pocus*, or my perennial favorite, *Pumpkinhead*. This is a great way to share the frights with your best fiends.

Head out to flea markets and antique shops for decor to creepify your crypt! A lot of what embodies the Gothic aesthetic are items that have a romantic, antiquated look, so what better place to search than in places where you can find items that are actually vintage and unique? The treasures you find may need a bit of help, due to their age, but you can use your DIY skills to restore a piece's true beauty.

Another wonderfully macabre way to spend an afternoon is at the local natural history museum, either with a pal or a trusty audio tour. When I was a child, I could roam the halls of New York's American Museum of Natural History for hours, completely enraptured by the dioramas of taxidermy animals. Spot a mummy or two in the Egyptian wing, and don't neglect the dinosaur skeletons, proof that giant monsters once roamed the Earth.

One of the most classic Gothic pastimes is the graveyard picnic. Beautiful stone crypts harken back to the Victorian ideal of *memento mori*, with extravagant, stately final resting places meant as a reminder of death's inevitability. Visit an old cemetery and you'll see weathered gravestones that hail to a more elegant time, when the process of mourning was accompanied by ornate sculptures, elegant fashion, and solemn rituals, and soak in the peace and tranquility of a beautifully maintained piece of land.

But before enjoying the surroundings, check the rules of your local graveyard. If eating is allowed, bring a blanket or just sit quietly on the grass and keep it low-key. Be sure to pick up all your rubbish and leave no trace that you were ever there. Don't play loud music or otherwise behave in a disrespectful manner. Always keep in mind that this is a place where people come to visit their dearly departed loved ones.

A graveyard picnic in Edinburgh, Scotland.

Make sure to also check the rules about photography. While it's typically allowed, some cemeteries might have rules against staging all-out photo shoots, so leave the tripod and lights at home. When taking photos in front of or next to crypts and tombstones, avoid capturing the name of the person buried there, out of respect for their family. No one wants to see photos online of some spooky vampires hanging upside down from their ancestor's final resting place.

I mean . . . *I* do. Maybe I'll even have it carved into my tombstone: *Here lies Aurelio Voltaire. Gothic photoshoots and graveyard picnics encouraged!*

But to be safe, you shouldn't assume others will want the same.

Painting the Town Black

If you want to have a night on the town, there are plenty of dark activities in which you might take part. To really get your blood pumping in the Halloween season, see if there is a haunt near you. In some haunts, the actors just jump out and scare you. At others, they may actually grab you. In some extreme cases, a haunt might offer intense experiences involving physical contact and *very* adult situations. Make sure the haunt you plan to attend is within your comfort level.

Horror lovers can also find horror conventions in their area. A convention is a great place to meet some of your favorite horror actors and hear them speak about their experiences. There are typically also vendors selling horror-themed wares, and sometimes activities like live music or dance parties. Take some friends or go make some new ones!

Whether you listen to post-punk, deathrock, Gothic rock, metal, or some other form of dark music, it's truly magic to see them perform live. If you've found that band that speaks to your soul, try to catch them on tour. Because most dark music genres don't appeal to the masses, these bands—especially the smaller ones—tend to be more in touch with their fans. They might run their own social media or work their own merchandise booths when they play in your town. I know I do! Buy some merch and they are likely to personally thank you for helping put gas in the van to get them to the next stop on the tour. I've been touring for over twenty years and there are long-time fans I see year after year at these shows that I now consider friends. It's all about community— connect with a stranger over a song you both love at a concert and you just might be making a spooky friend for life.

The single best place to go for a night of fun with like-minded ghouls is the local Goth night. Some might find walking into a dark room full of black-clad souls who like morbid music off-putting. But in my thirty or so years of attending Gothic events, I can say that I have never found a friendlier, more accepting group of people. While it might be a cliché that Goths are kids who were picked on in school and somehow found their way to this creepy scene, I can say that I often find it to be true. The part that many miss is that the bullying was typically due to being literate, intelligent, kind, creative, and other things that seemed "uncool" to the middle-school fools. Being bullied forces these sensitive souls to adopt a stance that most "normal" people are unkind and maybe even evil. Finding the Goth scene, they may begin to dress differently and listen to dark music, but they rarely stop being the sensitive souls they started out as. They eventually figure out there are places where people like them—like *us*—can congregate, so you end up with a room full of literate, intelligent, kind, and creative people . . . who just happen to be dressed like vampires. Uh, yes please!

One of the things I love most about Goth parties is that it is generally understood that Gothic dancing is a solitary sport. People go to swirl around to their favorite songs and let out whatever pent-up frustrations they might have. In most cases, people will leave you alone, if that is what you wish. And if someone asks you to dance, you can thank them for the offer and politely decline, and that will usually be that.

Goths, despite looking like blood-sucking ghouls, are typically extremely polite and respectful. I always say that in a regular bar, when a guy accidentally steps on another guy's foot, a fight will instantly break out. When a Goth guy steps on another Goth guy's pointy, skull-buckled boot, there is typically a race to apologize. And while there will always be one cranky edge lord insisting that you're "gothing wrong," know that the rest of us love you just the way you are!

When In Doubt . . .

A piece of advice about visiting a Goth night for the first time: wear all black! While that might seem superficial, there's actually a very practical reason for it. If you walk into a Goth club in khaki slacks and a brightly colored polo, Goths may think you are one of the normies who has come to the Goth club to bully and mock them (which, sadly, does sometimes happen). To avoid any confusion, simply wear black. You can show up in something as simple as a black T-shirt and black jeans. No one who matters will care if your outfit is expensive or not, fancy or plain. As long as it's all black, we can let our guard down knowing you're *one of us*.

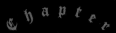

Chapter

12

Exploring Other People's Lives and Lairs

I'd like to believe that if you placed this book into the hands of a hundred different people, there would be a hundred different Gothic lairs created, each with its own distinctive look and character. It is important to me that you understand that *my* way is only *one* way of indulging in a macabre lifestyle and that my home is but one manifestation of these gloriously ghoulish ideas.

To prove that statement, I'd like to introduce you to a few of my friends. Each one of these beautiful souls is undoubtedly living their best Gothic life in their own glorious fashion and by their own rules. Each has created a gorgeously

PREVIOUS: A peek inside the home of Jade the Libra.

Gothic home for themselves, employing the color schemes and motifs that speak directly to them. And best of all, no two of these wonderful homes are alike!

Lawyer B. Douglas II of RavenWolf Manor

My dear friend Lawyer was born in Veracruz, Mexico, to a Mexican mother and a Black American father. He owes some of his spooky leanings to a superstitious upbringing: Catholicism, Curanderia, and Santeria on his mother's side and Baptist teachings and Voodoo practitioners on his father's. "I grew up afraid of the dark," he says, "all the while being attracted to it and curious of what secrets it held."

As a child, he was often told he did not belong. To escape a harsh world he describes as being "too noisy and too beige," he would create

The Bram Stoker's *Dracula* room at RavenWolf Manor.

fantasy worlds in which to find refuge. When imaginary places no longer sufficed, Lawyer began to create *real* places of comfort, teaching himself how to sew, paint, reupholster, make furniture, and more. Now, he uses these skills to show "that beauty can be found anywhere" and "that the monster we hide can be as beautiful as the prince we show."

Lawyer gets to do exactly that in the 133-year-old neoclassical Victorian manor he purchased in Navasota, Texas, about an hour outside Houston. This stately home is called RavenWolf Manor, and Lawyer has designs to invite the rest of the world into his creation when it opens as a darkly themed bed and breakfast and event space. I stayed in RavenWolf's Dracula Bedroom and felt like I'd become a character in a Gothic Victorian romance novel. There are also Edgar Allan Poe and *The Picture of Dorian Gray*-themed rooms. Lawyer says, "I want my home to always feel like the perfect autumn evening, so I decorate with rich dark colors like maroon, burnt orange, eggplant, bronze, and deep jewel tones." And though he loves black, Lawyer says, "I use it as a seasoning and not as the main course."

What makes this home so unique is that everything in it was made by Lawyer himself. "I only shop at thrift and vintage/antique stores," he says. "I cannot remember the last time I bought anything new. One of my favorite things to do is to give new life to discarded objects."

You can see more of the Manor on Instagram and TikTok at @pthearse.

Jade The Libra

In the Kansas City, Missouri, metro area lives my friend and fellow spooky YouTuber, Jade the Libra. Jade, who refers to herself as "a Midwest ghoul," shares her home with her husband and artistic partner, Dallas. They make music together as Shadow Figures and design clothing for their spooky brand, ho7s. Rounding out the beautifully spooky family are their son Lucian and their 18-year-old chihuahua, Neens.

Jade describes her home as being "nestled in a suburb where many of the houses look alike and the neighbors know you by name." She considered owning "an older home with lots of charm" but says, "we decided we could bring our darker taste into a 'cookie-cutter

home.'" Ultimately, they chose their home to be near her close-knit family. After all, it was her mother, a devoted *Dark Shadows* fan, who inspired her love for the macabre. Jade was born in October, which she credits for her "natural love for Halloween," adding, "I feel like I was born to love the strange and unusual."

I'd say Jade's sleek and stylish space borders on minimalism, which is a rarity! In the main living space, the walls are a very light gray, nearly white, with a perfectly polished wood floor between them. The Gothic is primarily communicated in the decor she carefully selects and displays on her mantel and shelves. "I decorate with a dark aesthetic all year round," she says, adding, "The variety of decorations and the meaning behind them contribute not only to a fun way to express myself, but also tells a spooky story to anyone daring to enter my home."

At Halloween, the elegant Jade isn't afraid to create what she calls "in your face Halloween themes" in her kitchen. "Halloween was always a magical time in our home with all the festive decor, the warm spicy scents of fall, and my Halloween-themed birthday parties," she explains. "My home is a representation of my nostalgic childhood and the ways in which Gothic styles continue to inspire me."

You can see how Jade's home has evolved on her YouTube channel, www.youtube.com/jadethelibra.

Goth Dad and the Tomb of Dusty's Doom

In Athens, Georgia, lives my spooky pal, Dusty Gannon, lead singer of the post-punk/goth rock band Vision Video. Dusty rose to internet fame as Goth Dad, a character he describes as "a wholesome midwestern vampire who teaches the 'baby bats' about the Goth subculture, cooking, makeup, and music."

Before creating Goth Dad, Dusty was a soldier and a firefighter. Born in Berlin, Germany, to a German mother and American father, the family moved a lot before settling in Georgia. As a young man he enlisted in the US Army and served as an infantry officer in Afghanistan. He left the service in 2016 and returned to Georgia, where he found work as a firefighter. Nowadays, Dusty is a full-time content creator and singer.

"Since my teenage years I've been deeply into Goth and post-punk music, as well as most horror films," Dusty explains. "I always took comfort in these darker forms of media and entertainment because I was a pretty weird kid and the strangeness of such really spoke to me."

An antique couch in Dusty's living room, found in Alabama by Dusty's partner, Scarlet. It brings a bit of classiness to the otherwise punk-rock vibe of the room.

That much is clear when you arrive at Dusty's home, or, as he calls it, the Tomb of Dusty's Doom. This single-story house on the edge of downtown Athens is approximately 120 years old and you can't miss it—it's painted black! If that doesn't help you find it, look for the black hearse parked in the driveway or the 12-foot skeleton (Skela Lugosi) standing out front.

The centerpiece of the all-black living room is a large, ornate, pumpkin-colored couch. The shelves are filled with horror DVDs and dark music albums. Dusty describes the vibe as "one part *The Return of the Living Dead*, one part *Interview with the Vampire,* and one part *Mister Rogers' Neighborhood*." The rest of the house is equally filled with horror movie posters, Halloween masks, creepy toys, and other in-your-face, horror-inspired decor. There's even an H.R. Giger, *Alien*-inspired tiki bar in the kitchen for making drinks of extraterrestrial strength. "I like to find the delicate balance of trashiness and class," Dusty says.

You can see more of Dusty's home on Instagram and TikTok at @VisionVideoBand.

Reby Hardy of House Hardy

For our next stop, we will drop in at a seven-bedroom house nestled in the middle of a forest in North Carolina. House Hardy is the stately home of Reby Hardy, former model, actress, radio host, and professional wrestler. These days she has her hands full raising four beautiful children, but still finds time to create content for her social media accounts as she travels the country promoting her book, *The Life of a Gothic Baby*.

Reby, who is of Puerto Rican heritage, married fellow professional wrestler Matt Hardy in 2013 and they've created a wonderfully spooky family and home. Their youngest child, Ever More, has become something of an internet celebrity through Reby's posts documenting the "Life of a Gothic Baby," which invite the

world into their extraordinary Gothic nursery and the rest of their majestic home. Reby says, "I want my home to make me feel like I'm a ghost in a Gothic romance novel. Floating around secret doorways and wood-carved banisters with a candelabra in hand. That's my goal."

With its dark walls and preponderance of candles and antiques, House Hardy has the feeling of a tidy and well-appointed haunted mansion. "To some, luxury means minimalism and a *clean* or beige aesthetic, but in my mind, it's all about the ornate," Reby says. "Gothic wood carvings and architecture, handwoven tapestries, and a worldly collection of antiques and oddities."

Since Reby heads a large family with varied tastes, it's not all doom and gloom! There are more colorful rooms for the children to play in, a video-game-themed room, and even a movie theater, where the family watches films and gathers to sing karaoke. You can see more of House Hardy and Gothic Baby on TikTok at @RebyHardy.

▲ A room fit for a Gothic Baby at House Hardy.

Ryan Matthew Cohn and Regina Marie Rossi

Ryan is a highly sought-after collector who specializes in rare and unusual antiques and artifacts related to science, anatomy, natural history, and memento mori. Along with wife Regina, who brings glamour and elegance to their exhibits and events, they are founders and producers of the Oddities Flea Market, a traveling high-end art market.

"I'd say we are your classic example of maximalism," says Ryan. "If there is space on a wall or surface, we tend to use it as a way to display and showcase our always-growing collection of rare artifacts and antiques."

The pair once lived in New York, but have now moved to a Connecticut home that can accommodate their immense and expanding collection. "We live in an ornate Victorian Italianate house dating to 1874," they say. "The estate comes complete with a matching cottage as well as an actual 'chapel' with spire. It is, of course, now painted black with stained windows and currently acts as a storage building for our overflow of antiques."

Their Oddities markets started in Brooklyn and have since expanded to include events in Los Angeles, Chicago, Seattle, Manhattan, and beyond. But what manner of objects might you see in their own home? "We specialize in fifteenth- to nineteenth-century decor and typically focus on the odd, unusual, and sometimes macabre. . . . We collect predominantly Old Master paintings, sculpture, drawings, prints, etc.," they say. "Most works are surrounded by the theme of death." Ryan and Regina have been inspired by their travel throughout Europe and visits to ancient cities, museums, and churches. "We tend to gravitate towards more Victorian color schemes such as deep reds, greens, etc., often using patterns and textures such as demask, velvets, and gilded/gold

accents." They find more of their rare and macabre pieces, from auction houses, European antique shops, antique shows, flea markets, and sometimes museums that are closing and selling their collections.

"We may not be your textbook Goths," they say, but, "we certainly do celebrate a dark aesthetic both in interior design and our fashion choices."

You can learn more about Ryan and Regina's collection and oddities markets at www.theodditiesfleamarket.com.

Just some of the stunning museum-worthy pieces that Ryan and Regina have collected.

I chose this particular collection of individuals not just because I happen to love them all dearly, but also because each of them has their own ideas on how to create a Gothic home. And now that you've seen the range and diversity of what's possible, what kind of Gothic home will you create?

A Final Note

My spooky friend, we've arrived at the end. I hope you've enjoyed flipping through these pages and have been inspired. It would make me very happy to know if our time together has entertained you for a while, and even happier to know if it has inspired you to pursue the spooky lifestyle you wish to live. Perhaps you've learned a dark DIY project perfect for your home, or picked up a delicious new recipe to try at your next Gothic get-together. If so, I hope you will share them with me by tagging me on social media so that I can see what you've created! I'm excited to witness how you've incorporated these tips into your own spooky life.

But most importantly, I hope this book has made one thing completely clear: that a Gothic life is for *anyone* who wishes it. It is for *you*, in fact, no matter what anyone might say to the contrary! One need not ask permission to enrich their lives by choosing to color their world with eerie aesthetics, macabre motifs, or spooky style. As it harms no one in the process, I say dive in! To quote *The Rocky Horror Picture Show*, "Don't dream it, be it!"

Anyone who loves and respects you—in other words, anyone who matters—will be absolutely delighted that you found something you love and will support you in your journey. And if you don't have anyone like that in your life, know that you have me now, and an amazingly supportive community of like-minded souls.

If I've learned anything in the several decades I've spent on this planet, it's that life is far too short to keep yourself from following your

A final skull to send you on your way.

heart for fear of what others might think or say. Many might find it ironic that painting your world black is what brings a smile to your face, but in a world full of darkness (the bad kind, not the kind we know and love!), joy is sometimes in short supply, so it's important that we grab it where and when we can. I hope that, with this book, I've helped bring a cemetery smile to your spooky face.

And I hope to see that smile in person! Come see me when I perform my Halloween hits and dark ditties near you. I'm almost constantly on tour, so come to a show and say hello. I want to see how your lair is coming along and know that you're happy, and I want to hear about how you are living your best Gothic life!

There is much more to come in the way of dark decorating tips, spooky shopping, and terrifying travel tips on *Gothic Homemaking*, so I hope you'll tune in and add your two cents in the comments. Let's continue to support each other as you and I continue on our journey to be authentically ourselves.

As always, stay spooky!

Voltaire

Acknowledgments

While this humble book may seem quite small in your hand, it contains what amounts to three or four years' worth of *Gothic Homemaking* episodes, had I created them for the show instead of for this book. It goes without saying that I would never have been able to accomplish this feat in such a short time without a tremendous amount of help. For starters, I must thank Roberto Beltran and his assistant, Alejandra Sánchez, who came up from Mexico to shoot nearly all the incredible photographs you see in this book! For over two weeks, they worked insanely long hours with nary a complaint, even when we had to extend their stay twice to get everything finished.

Our on-set art department consisted of only one person besides me, and that was Gerrold Vincent, whose enthusiasm and artistic skills are apparently endless! It would have been impossible for me to have made every single prop in the time allotted, but luckily, I had some very talented people lend a hand. My former stop-motion student, Peter Keehn, made me proud with the incredible work he did on the Pumpkin King figure, Midnight Moon Bakery was super sweet to help with the cookies, and I was over the moon to be able to have my favorite YouTubers, Wicked Makers, tackle the Spooky Scary Skeleghost. If you're not already subscribed to their channel on YouTube, please do so immediately!

My fiancée, Mayumi Toyoda, helped with the DIY projects that required sewing skills beyond my own. But her emotional support is what I'm most grateful for, as without it, I would have never made it to the end of this project with my sanity intact.

¡Y un enorme agradecimiento a la familia Toyoda por permitirme realizar las tomas de SummerWeen en su patio en México cuando todavía era invierno en la ciudad de Nueva York!

Big thanks to my favorite tiki bar, the Golden Tiki in Las Vegas, for the awesome skull mug, to Von Payne Spirits for the epic elixir, to Dellamorte and Co. for making sure Creepy Christmas had plenty of Krampus, to Killstar for helping me spill the tea in spooky style, and to my friends Zach and Cameron at Beetle House in NYC for giving me a spooky place to host a frightful feast (in Chapter 7), when the Lair was too small to handle it. And a huge hug to my friends Lawyer, Jade, Dusty, Reby, Ryan, and Regina, who graciously allowed me to welcome you into their homes!

Most importantly, enormous thanks to the team at Quarto and Epic Ink for believing in this project and for guiding me towards its fruition.

And of course, thank you for giving this book a chance! I'm humbled by your enthusiasm and support. In my darkest hours, I always know that I'll get by with a little help from my fiends!

About the Author

Often described as a modern-day renaissance man, **Aurelio Voltaire** is an accomplished singer-performer, author, and creator of films, animation, toys, and home decor.

As an internationally touring musician for nearly 30 years, Voltaire is at the forefront of the Gothic and Dark Cabaret genres. Mixing mirth with the macabre, his music becomes increasingly sought after around Halloween. Walk through a Spirit Halloween and you're bound to hear some of his songs from the Cartoon Network show, *The Grim Adventures of Billy and Mandy*. Voltaire has released 13 full-length studio albums, as well as a collection of his Halloween hits.

When not touring or recording, Voltaire can be seen in his informative and hilarious YouTube series, *Gothic Homemaking*. Like a young Vincent Price taking over for Martha Stewart, he demonstrates how to turn a boring home into a Gothic lair. *The New York Times* published a feature on Voltaire, calling him, "The Martha Stewart for Macabre Homemakers" and "a lifestyle guru to people who embrace spookiness in all seasons."

Gothic Homemaking can be seen on YouTube @TheLairofVoltaire. For more information about Voltaire's music, books, touring schedule, and more, visit his official website at voltaire.net.

First published in 2024 by Epic Ink, an imprint of The Quarto Group,
142 West 36th Street, 4th Floor, New York, NY 10018, USA
(212) 779-4972 • www.Quarto.com

Epic Ink titles are also available at discount for retail, wholesale, promotional, and bulk purchase. For details, contact the Special Sales Manager by email at specialsales@quarto.com or by mail at The Quarto Group, Attn: Special Sales Manager, 100 Cummings Center Suite 265D, Beverly, MA 01915 USA.

10 9 8 7 6 5 4 3 2

ISBN: 978-0-7603-8832-7

Digital edition published in 2024
eISBN: 978-0-7603-8833-4

Library of Congress Control Number: 2024932673

Group Publisher: Rage Kindelsperger
Senior Acquisitions Editor: Nicole James
Creative Director: Laura Drew
Senior Art Director: Marisa Kwek
Managing Editor: Cara Donaldson
Editor: Katie McGuire
Cover Design: Marisa Kwek
Interior Design: Silverglass

Photography: Roberto Beltran, except where noted; Aurelio Voltaire: 178, 180, 182, 183, 185 *bottom*, 192, 194 *top*, 195, 196, 197; Lawyer B. Douglas: 194 *bottom*; Reby Hardy: 198, 199; David Zeck: 200, 201; Getty Images: 16 (Charlie Gillett Collection), 18 (John Kisch Archive), 19 (Watal Asanuma/Shinko Music), 20 *top* (MPI/Stringer), 20 *bottom* (Silver Screen Collection), 23 (Archive Photos/Stringer), 181 *top* (John Coletti), 181 *bottom* (Universal Images Group), 184 (TravelCouples), 185 *top* (Agung Parameswara/ Stringer/Getty Images AsiaPac), 186 *bottom* (Maremagnum), 187 *top* (Adam Berry), 187 *bottom* (Danny Lawson - PA Images); Alamy Stock Photo: 21 (Netflix/FlixPix), 22 (Moviestore Collection), 24 (AJ Pics), 50 (Panther Media), 186 *top* (Cols Travel), 189 (Jurgen Wiesler); Shutterstock: 126, 136

Printed in China